RETHINKING ON MICROFINANCE

Edited by

Dr. N.A. MUJUMDAR

Dr. M.G. SHIRAHATTI

Himalaya Publishing House

MUMBAI • NEW DELHI • NAGPUR • BENGALURU • HYDERABAD • CHENNAI • PUNE • LUCKNOW • AHMEDABAD • ERNAKULAM • BHUBANESWAR • INDORE • KOLKATA • GUWAHATI

First Edition : 2011

Published by : Mrs. Meena Pandey for **Himalaya Publishing House Pvt. Ltd.,** "Ramdoot", Dr. Bhalerao Marg, Girgaon, **Mumbai - 400 004.** Phone: 022-23860170/23863863, Fax: 022-23877178 **E-mail: himpub@vsnl.com; Website: www.himpub.com**

Branch Offices :

New Delhi : "Pooja Apartments", 4-B, Murari Lal Street, Ansari Road, Darya Ganj, New Delhi - 110 002. Phone: 011-23270392, 23278631; Fax: 011-23256286

Nagpur : Kundanlal Chandak Industrial Estate, Ghat Road, Nagpur - 440 018. Phone: 0712-2738731, 3296733; Telefax: 0712-2721215

Bengaluru : No. 16/1 (Old 12/1), 1st Floor, Next to Hotel Highlands, Madhava Nagar, Race Course Road, Bengaluru - 560 001. Phone: 080-32919385; Telefax: 080-22286611

Hyderabad : No. 3-4-184, Lingampally, Besides Raghavendra Swamy Matham, Kachiguda, Hyderabad - 500 027. Phone: 040-27560041, 27550139; Mobile: 09848130433

Chennai : No. 85/50, Bazullah Road, T. Nagar, Chennai - 600 017. Phone: 044-28144004/28144005

Pune : First Floor, "Laksha" Apartment, No. 527, Mehunpura, Shaniwarpeth (Near Prabhat Theatre), Pune - 411 030. Phone: 020-24496323/24496333

Lucknow : Jai Baba Bhavan, Church Road, Near Manas Complex and Dr. Awasthi Clinic, Aliganj, Lucknow - 226 024. Phone: 0522-2339329, 4068914; Mobile: 09305302158, 09415349385, 09389593752

Ahmedabad : 114, "SHAIL", 1st Floor, Opp. Madhu Sudan House, C.G. Road, Navrang Pura, Ahmedabad - 380 009. Phone: 079-26560126; Mobile: 09327324149, 09314679413

Ernakulam : 39/104 A, Lakshmi Apartment, Karikkamuri Cross Rd., Ernakulam, Cochin - 622011, Kerala. Phone: 0484-2378012, 2378016; Mobile: 09344199799

Bhubaneswar : 5 Station Square, Bhubaneswar (Odisha) - 751 001. Mobile: 09861046007

Indore : Kesardeep Avenue Extension, 73, Narayan Bagh, Flat No. 302, IIIrd Floor, Near Humpty Dumpty School, Narayan Bagh, Indore - 452 007 (M.P.). Mobile: 09301386468

Kolkata : 108/4, Beliaghata Main Road, Near ID Hospital, Opp. SBI Bank, Kolkata - 700 010, Phone: 033-32449649, Mobile: 09910440956

Guwahati : House No. 15, Behind Pragjyotish College, Near Sharma Printing Press, P.O. Bharalumukh, Guwahati - 781009. (Assam). Mobile: 09883055590, 09883055536

DTP by : HPH, Editorial Office, Bhandup (Nalini & Megha)

Printed by : Print Home, Mumbai.

Acknowledgements

I would like to express my gratitude to all the eminent and distinguished experts who cordially accepted my invitation and took some time off their busy schedule to participate in the seminar. Their participation went a long way in making this seminar a grand success.

My sincere thanks and appreciation to Dr. N.A. Mujumdar, Former Principal Advisor, RBI and Professor Emeritus for his sincere help in compilation of this book.

I also appreciate Dr. Menon Shreedharan who invested a lot of effort and energy in compilation of this book. He played an active role in collection of research papers from all the dignitaries and he was also instrumental in organizing the seminar. I value his immense contribution.

I would like to compliment our Administrative Officer Mr Sanoj Kumar and all the administrative staff who were of great help in terms of logistics and organization of the seminar.

I would also like to thank Prof. Raghavendra for his contribution in the proceedings of the seminar and compilation of this book.

I am also thankful to Mr. Vaibhav Pol who transcribed and typed the entire material.

I am also very grateful to Mr. Pandey of Himalaya Publishing House who at my personal request readily agreed to publish the Volume.

Dr. M.G Shirahatti
(Director General, OIM)

February 2011
Oriental Institute of Management and
Oriental School of Business,
Vashi, Navi Mumbai.

...About the Authors

- Dr. Abhay Pethe: Director, Dept. of Economics, University of Mumbai, Kalina
- Dr. N.A. Mujumdar: Former Adviser, RBI
- Dr. S.L. Khumbhare: CGM, MCID, NABARD
- Miss. Nidhi Chandra and Dr. R.K. Pattnaik: Senior Professor, SIMSR
- Dr. C.L. Dadhich: Secretary, Indian Society of Agricultural Economics
- Mrs. Vijaya Venkatesh: Director, Research Division, ISAE
- Mr. Shariar Karim: Corporate Trainer
- Mr. Abhishek Chokshi: Vice President, Matrix Financial Consultants Ltd.
- Mr. Raghavendra S. Bendigeri: Assistant Professor, Oriental Institute of Management, Navi Mumbai
- Mr. N.C. Khulbe: GM, Priority Sector, Bank of India
- Dr. Minoo Thomas: Principal, SIES College, Sion, Mumbai
- Shri Hemanth Kumar: Group Vice President, BASIX
- Mr. Chetnanda Rao: Group Vice President, Hindhustan Micro Finance Pvt. Ltd.
- Mrs. Radhika HariBhakti: Director, Spandana Micro Finance Ltd.
- Mr. A.N. Wankhade: Deputy Manager, Maharashtra State Cooperative Bank, Sector 17, Vashi
- Mr. S. Chandrasekhar: Senior Faculty, PNB Staff Training College, Belapur, Navi Mumbai

...Table of Contents

...Case Studies

...Appendix

Introduction

Dr. Shirahatti's choice of the Seminar theme was timely. One of the papers presented at the Seminar had "looming crisis" as part of its title. This proved to be prophetic. The promulgamation of Andhra Governments Ordinance on Micro Finance triggered the crisis and the rest is history. So, many unsavioury aspects of the functioning of for-profit Micro Finance Institutions (MFls) which attracted little attention hitherto, came to light.

More recent revelations of for-profit Micro Finance Institutions (MFIs) have exposed how these institutions are exploiting the situation in the name of financial inclusion. In addition to the usurious lending rates of 30 to 40 per cent, the Managing Directors of some of the bigger MFIs were paid obscenely high remuneration packages of say Rs. 4 crore to Rs. 8 crore — the level higher than that of Managing Director of HDFC Bank. There was also no transparency in the mutual benefit trusts (MBTs) — the shareholding vehicle for MFIs (*Economic Times Investigations*). Perhaps, the last nail in the coffin of these for-profit MFIs was hit by the recent statement of Dr. V.Y. Reddy, former Governor, Reserve Bank of India (RBI), that for-profit MFIs are worse than moneylenders. Moneylender lends out of his own money, whereas here, MFIs were actually borrowing money from depositors and banks and on lending the money. So, "MFI is essentially a leveraged moneylender" (*Economic Times*, 23 November, 2010). He went on further to add that many finance experts believed, but did not have the courage to admit publicly, that, micro finance is India's subprime: "Ultimately, it is something like subprime lending". The studied silence of experts has cost the economy a great deal, as we will see. In retrospect, the Government of Andhra Pradesh deserves to be congratulated on its ordinance issued in 2010 which spelt out clearly the malpractices of such MFIs: "Whereas these SHGs are being exploited by private Micro Finance Institutions (MFIs) through usurious interest rates and coercive means of recovery resulting in their impoverishment and in some cases leading to suicides....." This triggered a crisis which almost paralysed for-profit MFIs, with banks reluctant to lend, 'repayments dwindling and depositors tending to withdraw their money'. It is this shock therapy which led to subsequent soul-searching on the part of those MFIs the promoters of which were fattening themselves on the sweat of the poor borrowers. The Micro Finance Institutions Network (MFIN), a grouping of for-profit microlenders, has now set up a Committee to look into these deficiencies. In fact, the clout of these MFI seems to be so strong that in spite of all that has been now exposed, some influential papers plead: "Don't kill Micro Finance". The short answer to such pleas is: "We do not want to kill these MFIs; but we certainly want to prevent them from killing their poor borrowers".

No doubt, the for-profit MFIs represent the predatory face of financial capitalism. But this was compounded by the institutional support which was extended to these MFIs. Such support came from Reserve Bank of India (RBI), public sector banks (PSBs), NABARD and SIDBI. For instance, during 2008-09, banks extended loans of something like Rs. 3700 crore. Why should PSBs extend loans to MFIs at something like 12 per cent, when they were fully aware that these funds would be on-lent by MFIs at 25 to 30 per cent? The answer is that such loans by PSBs to MFIs were treated as priority sector lending. So this had the blessings of RBI. Similarly, some equity or quasi-equity support came from SIDBI and NABARD, of course, at concessional rates. RBI could have stipulated that PSBs should lend only to "not-for-profit category" of MFIs. PSBs could have also stipulated, on their part, that the onlending rate of beneficiary MFIs should not 'exceed say 17 or 18 per cent'. This was not done. This systemic support perhaps also lent some respectability to for-profit MFIs. Thus, public sector financial resources were used to perpetuate usurious lending practices of MFIs.

In all humility, we may ask Dr. Reddy: It is one thing to say that RBI had no statutory powers to regulate MFIs; but was it obliged to support for-profit MFIs? RBI could have stipulated that PSBs should lend only to not-for-profit MFIs, fixing a ceiling on their onlending rates. This support made the system, in a manner of speaking, a coconspirator in this business of exploiting poor rural borrowers. Public funds were allowed to generate private profits. RBI has not covered itself in glory in this episode.

The sordid story does not end here. Because of high returns, some may even say obscenely high returns, stemming from exorbitant lending rates, for-profit MFIs have become attractive investment destinations for Private Equity and Venture Capitalists. The recent success of IPA of SKS Micro finance is a case in point. It attracted high profile investors like billionaire George Soros, venture capitalist Vinod Khosala and Infosys Founder Narayan Murthy. Alluding to this transformation of the humble animal micro finance, Muhammad Yunus, the father of micro finance movement said: "It is a complete detour and nothing but a quitting of micro finance mission". The original micro finance concept of helping the poor via small loans at reasonable rates of interest has been abdicated (*Economic Times*, 13th December, 2010). Is it a case of Shylocks masquerading as micro finance institutions? One wonders.

Basically, lending to the rural poor at 30 or 40 per cent defies all economic logic. Our small rural borrowers are not Schumpeterian mini-heroes, who can make the project or activity for financing what they have borrowed, financially viable. In fact, by inflating interest cost, we are building *ab in tio* non-viability into the project. Secondly, the engagement of for-profit MFIs with borrowers has been shallow based on "touch and move" on business models shorn of any development content. "The average loans per client in both MFIs and SHGs have been low, between Rs. 3500 and Rs. 5000. The duration of the loan is short, typically one year or less. The small loan size and short duration do not enable most borrowers to do much except to ease liquidity problems". (Micro Finance India: State of the Sector Report, 2008). It was M.L. Darling who wrote long ago that the Indian peasant is born in debt, lives in debt and dies in debt, thanks to the moneylender. Are we trying to promote the Darling syndrome?

It should be underlined that the policymakers' indifference to exorbitant rural lending rates is in sharp contrast to their concern for corporate sector. Whenever RBI even contemplates raising of repo rates by say 0.25 per cent, the corporate lobby is up in arms. Don't raise lending rates, it will hurt growth. More often than not, RBI yields to the corporate sector plea.

Whatever RBI's Malegam Committee has recommended, covers some ground towards reforming the for-profit MFIs. But it seems to have missed the central point. The public sector support to for-profit MFIs should be withdrawn forthwith. After all, why did PSBs begin to extend their support to such MFIs? Because these MFIs provided 'an easy escape route' to their responsibility regarding meeting the priority sector credit target of 40 per cent. In doing so, we have landed ourselves into a greater mess. Then there was this facade of financial inclusion. This empirical experience has demonstrated that under such circumstances it is better not to have borrowed at all, at prohibitive costs, than borrowed and lost. It is better to remain "excluded" than "included".

Where do we go from here? Indian policymakers must be reminded that India, unlike many other countries like Bangladesh, for example, has a healthy home-grown segment of micro finance. Public Sector Banks (PSBs), restructured Regional Rural Banks (RRBs) rejuvenated cooperative credit system, NABARD's Self-help Groups (SHGs)-Bank Linkage Programme (SBLP), which has emerged as a major channel of micro finance. Then there is the Post Office, which is already functioning as a semi-bank, with its 1.55 lakh branches and some 16 crore customers. This has great potential, given appropriate policy support, to emerge as a low-cost micro finance channel. The point is that these public or semi-public sector segments have successfully blended profitability criteria with social banking. Of course, "nor-for-profit" MFIs are indeed welcome to join the stream. Our policymakers could do well to refocus their energies on further developing this segment, rather than trying to reform rouge MFIs. In the business of financial inclusion, there is enough space for not-for-profit MFIs but not for rogue MFIs.

This book which contains the papers presented as well as the presentations, offers a rich fare. There are analytical studies of aspects of functioning of MFIs and there are some case studies. We do hope that this book will provoke informed thinking on the subject. Probably, it will also provide some inputs to policy makers now engaged in reshaping the MFIs.

February, 2011.

N.A. Mujumdar

1 Rethinking on Micro Finance in the Current Scenario*

Prof. Dr. Abhay Pethe,
Director, Dept. of Economics, UOM, Kalina

Rethinking on Micro Finance in the Current Scenario*

- Thank you for having me here this morning and let me begin by congratulating the Oriental Institute for organizing this National Seminar on this very pertinent topic at this opportune time.

  In this brief intervention, I propose to begin by setting out my understanding/ perception of the context provided by the broad macroeconomic environment prevailing in our country at the moment and then go on to underline the importance of micro finance. I will then flag some issues related to micro finance practices and institutions proper as they are evolving in our country.

- Let me now share my perception/understanding of the 'current context' which provides the parametric framework to my discussion. Indian growth story is by now well-known and documented. There is also a fair consensus that this growth story has an unmistakable exclusionary sub-plot. The exclusion manifests itself variously in terms sectors, activities, groups of people and geographical spaces (rural/urban/states). There is a clear recognition at the highest level of policy making that this has to be negated or else all will be lost. At the most visible level, we see this reflected in the 11th FYP (Five Year

* Inaugural Address delivered by Dr. Abhay Pethe, Director, Department of Economics (Autonomous), University of Mumbai, in the National Seminar on "Rethinking on Micro Finance in the Current Scenario" organized by Oriental Institute of Management, Plot No. 149, Sector 12, Vashi, Navi Mumbai, on 24th and 25th Sept., 2010.

Plan) which has inclusion as the central focus. There are indications that the 12th FYP (Five Year Plan) will be expected to continue with the focus and flesh it out with a renewed emphasis on skill set development. The lesson here is that whilst growth is good in that it swells the treasury, it does so in an asymmetric fashion with the Central Government turning out to be the chief beneficiary. The constitutionally mandated responsibilities with the States and the curb on revenue expenditure (even the 'good' type) induced by FRBMA (Fiscal Responsibility and Budget Management Act) and FRLs has led to a real scarcity of resources putting an undue stress on State government offers.

❖ On the other hand and in contrast, in order to inject basic developmental components such as education and healthcare requires substantial resources at the State government level. Thus, we come up against a road block. The discretionary fiscal space with the States has been reducing monotonically over the last several years. This has to do with the constitutional mandate on the one hand and the tax arrangements in place. Of course, with the 'grand bargain' in the form of GST (Government Service Tax) soon to be unveiled, it is to be hoped that the States' problem may be somewhat alleviated.

❖ One of the obvious consequences of the above has been that the Central Government is sitting on a huge pile of resources and consequently there has been a huge boost to the now familiar Centrally Sponsored Schemes (CSSs). Apart from logistical difficulties associated with financial flows (given the governance process), there is an obvious intrusion on the State Government's autonomy that has led to a debate and a relook at the fiscal federal structure prevalent in our country. More importantly, the CSS funds apart from being tied and revenue type, can only work as short-term temporary palliatives (however important and essential they may be) and would fall short in solving the problem of empowerment of the vulnerable members of our society. To be sure, the policy makers that frame such policies in a Keynesian mould are most probably aware of this.

❖ With the skill sets required by the new growth process and the relatively low growth in employment expected, this empowerment has to come via the credit enhancement to the poor and the vulnerable. The 'western understanding' and practice of good banking/finance and the associated risk valuation means that most of such poor will not be entertained by our formal financial system. As my friend and mentor, Dr. N.A. Mujumdar, has persuasively argued, there is a need to learn/understand the concept of 'composite credit' and restructure the risk matrix on part of our formal financial institutions and agents. As an aside I may say that whilst I am not totally convinced by his almost pathological distaste for 'western capitalism' and its financial practices, I am convinced to suitably modify our ways in a MARK II fashion even whilst remaining within the ambit of what I can broadly term as 'market-driven' ethos with its attendant discipline. This then is the context and premise of financial inclusion on which micro finance becomes crucial.

❖ Let me begin with the International scenario. United Nations has taken upon itself of the task of poverty reduction and improvement of life of poor by reducing poverty to half by 2015. Transformational development is aimed at by organizations like Consultative Group to assist the Poor, Grameen, Worldvision, Seva who have advocated complete codes of beliefs and living; and their results are apparent through dedicated people-centric service. They provide a range of interventions tailored to the context in a holistic manner. This means providing livelihood capabilities whilst at once taking care of basic needs such as elementary education and healthcare. This is with local staffing, bank services, rural outreach centers, trust groups, technological innovations through dynamic, dedicated, social or professional teams.

❖ Micro Finance Institutions (MFIs for short) offer a variety of products, including loans, savings, micro insurance, training, support, guidance, encouragement tailored to poor communities to improve their lives through their work. Sources of funds for the micro finance organizations are donations, bank loans, and government funds amongst others. Micro finance activities started with development projects involving local/foreign aid projects by NGOs with some government support/intervention. Presently, they operate as any of the following legal entities: Trusts, NGOs, Banks, Non-Banking Financial Institutions, Rural Banks, Cooperatives, Credit unions, companies, etc. Worldwide, there are more than 1,000 micro finance companies as of 2008. Micro finance institutions currently operate in over 100 countries, serving more than 75 million clients, more than 70% ladies (some exclusively or, even 98%). Many MFIs offer services beyond loans and savings, including education on business and financial issues and social services focused on health and children. The loans are used to run their occupation and earn a living. Some buy livestock; a sewing machine and fabric to make clothes and accessories, inventory for a local store; a tractor or seed and other farming equipment and supplies, food shops. The possibilities are endless as to what a micro entrepreneur can do with the loan. Micro finance clients have excellent track records for repayment. Repayment rates for micro finance loans on a global level average about 97 per cent. Thus, a lot can be learnt from this, the fact remains that in India given the sheer magnitude of the problem much more needs to be done.

- In India, the micro finance portfolio and outreach has been increasing through two channels: SHG-Linked Program (SBLP) and MFIs. Although the coverage is still variously estimated, the fact is that compared to the untapped number of poor families in the country it is still miniscule and a lot needs to be done. The growth rates in recent times (08, 09) at around 30% and 55% respectively for MFIs and SBLP is quite impressive. Although the concentrated localization in terms of banks (only 4 SBI and 3 southern banks) as well as in spatial sense is a negative feature in terms of presence the coverage has shown considerable increase. The industry is estimated to expand its portfolio to 200,000 crore INR by 2015.

- There is an emerging trend in micro finance arena with professional 'for profit' MFIs set to play an ever increasing role. The recent IPO of SKS finance is a case in point. One is seeing a lot of bad press with questions being asked about the social commitment, profit motive, cherry picking *et al.* The fact of the matter is that SKS has a market share of 21 per cent and a huge spatial coverage and a track record that shows 99% performance on loan return matter. Also in the MFI space, there appears to be too many players who are too small and appear unable to scale. This is going to inevitably lead to messy takeovers and mergers. This could well cause some concern.

- Whilst some of the above criticism might have substance and others might frown at this trend for ethical reasons, I am convinced that if we have proper oversight from a distance, this market-driven attribute can only do good and all indicators are that they are already delivering (witness the multiple loans taking by agents which was not a feature of government backed schemes). This can only introduce the concept of viability (however modified) into this activity. Perhaps, the pioneers who were inspired by the idea to do good (no sarcasm intended) must seriously introspect if they can learn something from the 'johnnies come lately' as if at all their criticism is inspired due to the perception of their turf being threatened.

- The loan losses of MFIs are very low at about 1-2% but the real concern is with the root cause of such defaults which can be treated only by building of social collateral (extending the idea of SHGs). The MF faces a host of challenges such as reduction of the resource costs that are too high except that the alternative is even costlier. The governmental regulation need to be made more non-intrusive (although with tough supervision and teeth) as well as user-friendly with embedded incentives. The holistic nature of activities mean that a host of professional trainers (apart from financial) with much motivation are required within the core team and this has cost implications. As does the very nature of activity which is doorstep/extension delivery. The NBFC status needs a relook and whether the RBI will allow limited banking activity on part of MFIs needs to be explored. The 'bill' which has not seen the light of the day due to concern of conflict of interest has to be passed thereby clarifying the legal status. The current talk about the RBI considering MFIs to function as official for profit BCs is a step forward.

- There is great scope for improving the micro finance programme in India provided we take care of some of the pressing concerns such as:
  - For micro finance institutions to be sustainable in the long run, they need to expand their resource base. The resource base for most is largely comprised of loans from commercial banks and corporate funding. There is a need to explore new ways to increase resource base by accessing the debt market (not junk grade) or equity market (as is already happening).
  - A provision for setting up a refinance facility that could act as a last resort facility for MFIs needs to be made.
  - Micro finance programme in India needs to expand its reach if it has to make a dent in solving the problem of financial exclusion of the poor. It needs to expand its networks and a collaboration of informal micro finance organizations with their formal sector counterparts such as commercial banks could work to serve this purpose. Such a joint venture would draw on the strengths of both the formal and informal organizations; the former would be better equipped to provide resources as they have a wide resource base while the latter have an advantage in terms of more information regarding the poor and vulnerable groups and can serve as intermediaries between borrowers and formal financial sector.
  - Such partnerships could also lead to borrowers getting access to credit at lower rates of interest. This is because the monitoring and enforcement costs of commercial banks would be lowered if they were to rely on informal

sector NGO-MFIs and they would then be willing to lend to the poor. The poor would thus get access to loans at rates that are slightly higher than the formal sector lending rates (the difference between this interest rate and formal rates would accrue to the informal sector MFI) but lower than the conventional rates of 24-36% charged by the MFIs.

— There is tremendous demand for housing finance among the poorer sections. Housing loans are provided by the formal sector at 9.25%. If the formal lending was to extend to the poorer sections, monitoring and enforcements costs would have to be incurred which would push up the lending rate to say 12%. This is still much lower than the MFI lending rate of 18-20%.

— The working of micro finance in India needs to become more flexible and adaptive. Introducing flexibility in period of repayment would reduce stress on households. Also, the credit packages offered to the poor need to be more flexible and serve the multiple credit requirements of the borrowers (which include consumption, employment generation and others). The condition of compulsory savings should be modified to allow depositors to withdraw up to after a certain threshold of savings has been reached.

❖ Thus, there is a great possibility of using micro finance as a tool for fostering inclusion via empowerment of the poor and the vulnerable. The need here arises not only out of ethical and moral consideration (although they are not bad motives either) but through hard-headed analysis backed by pragmatic considerations. This is one opportunity we must not miss or else the very integration of our polity and society will be in danger through the socio-economic strife that will surely ensue!

❖ Thank you for your time and patience.

■■■

2 Macroeconomic Policy Mix and Micro Finance Institutions

Dr. N.A. Mujumdar,
Former Adviser, RBI

Macroeconomic Policy Mix and Micro Finance Institutions

Originally, micro finance was conceived as a sort of philanthropic movement designed to provide, on a small scale, cheap credit to the most needy. Micro Credit was inspired by the development philosophy since it was regarded as the most innovative strategy to address global poverty. Alas! this is no longer so. Internationally, micro finance as an institution is at crossroads. This is reflected in the following question posed by Andrew Hilton, Director, Centre for the Study of Financial Innovation: "Should micro finance institutions shift from their essential social role to (perhaps) more sustainable profit-seeking model?[1] "Perhaps, an element of guilt conscience is gnawing those pioneers of micro finance about this journey of micro finance from "not for profit" to essentially a commercial model.

Indian micro finance institutions (MFIs) do not seem to have any qualms about such transformation. During more recent years, they have made rapid strides both in terms of coverage of clients or customers and in terms of quantum of credit extended. This has raised high expectations about the role they can play in financial inclusion and poverty reduction. They also seem to have taken the Indian policy makers for a ride, as is reflected in the support they have received from the public sector financial institutions.

I would seek to show in my brief address, that the commercial model of MFIs is ill-suited to our objectives of financial inclusion or inclusive growth in the real sector.

An objective analysis of the functioning of the commercial model of MFIs shows that they have emerged as essentially glorified moneylenders, charging usurious lending rates of 30 to 40 per cent to the poor borrowers. Because of high returns, some even say obscenely high returns, stemming from exorbitant lending rates, MFIs have become attractive investment destinations for Private Equity and Venture Capitalists.[2] Questions about who gets rich and how rich by selling financial services to the poor are now being raised. What a transformation!

What is perhaps more disturbing is that the macroeconomic policy mix relating to financial sector reforms is flawed in the sense that it has supported such transformation. Are we trying to promote the so-called Darling Syndrome? It was M.L. Darling who wrote long ago that the Indian peasant is born in debt, lives in debt and dies in debt, thanks to the moneylender! We should remember that our small borrowers are not Schumpeterian mini-heores, who can make the project or activity for the financing which they have borrowed at 30 or 40 per cent, financially viable. In fact by inflating the interest-cost, we are building, *ab in itio*, non-viability into the project. SIDBI's Impact Assessment Study of micro finance programmes clearly reveals this point: "A large number of clients (32 per cent) considered interest charged on loan too high and wanted it to be reduced".[3] What is rather intriguing is that although the SIDBI Report provides some success stories in the form of "Boxes", it studiously avoids giving the actual rates of interest charged on loans. Is SIDBI shy of disclosing these embarrassingly high lending rates? Even the imperatives of financial inclusion, as we will show shortly, do not justify such high rates. One could argue that, under such circumstances, it is better not to have borrowed at all, at prohibitive costs, than borrowed and lost. It is the business of micro finance institutions to provide affordable credit: not Shylock's credit. Perhaps, only speculative activities could yield adequate returns after absorbing such high interest costs. Although MFIs show high recovery ratios, recently, apprehensions are being expressed in some quarters about the sustainability of the system. Has the recent fast rate of growth of MFIs led to the formation of a bubble waiting to burst?

Finally, Indian policy makers must be reminded that India, unlike many other countries like Bangladesh for example, has a healthy home-grown segment of micro finance. Public Sector Banks (PSBs), restructured Regional Rural Banks (RRBs), rejuvenated cooperative credit system: NABARD's Self-help Group-Bank Linkage Programme (SBLP), which has emerged as a major channel of micro finance. Then there is the Post Office, which is already functioning as a semi-bank, with its 1.55 lakh branches and some 16 crore customers. This has a great potential, given appropriate policy support, to emerge as a low-cost micro finance channel. The point is that these public or semi-public sector segments have successfully blended profitability criteria with social banking. Our policy makers could do well to refocus their energies on this segment rather than support directly or indirectly this new breed of glorified moneylenders.

At this stage, for conceptual clarity, some explanation is warranted. In India we have two main channels of micro finance: the SHG-Bank Linkage Programme (SBLP) of NABARD and Micro Finance Institutions (MFIs). Under the former, loans of some Rs.12,250 crore were disbursed through 16.1 million Self-help Groups in 2008-09. Banking sector has also been extending loans to MFIs for onlending to SHGs. During 2008-09, bank loans amounting to Rs. 3,732 crore were disbursed to 581 MFIs. The total loans outstanding rose to Rs. 5,009 crore to 1,915 MFIs at the end of March 2009. Within the MFIs again, there are two broad categories: "Not for Profit" and "For Profit". There is a strong lobby that the "For Profit", or shall we say, only "For Profit" category can play an important role in financial inclusion. The theme of this address focuses on this category.

The central question is: if traditional moneylenders are subjected to ceiling on their lending rates, why should the glorified moneylenders — the "For Profit" MFIs — be exempt from interest cap, especially when they have shed their social banking responsibility? This category of MFIs has today drained themselves of any development content. Our financial sector reformers have not covered themselves in glory as their track record shows. They will be adding to their list of mistakes, if such a ceiling on lending rates of commercial MFIs is not imposed. Of course, the Micro Financial Sector (Development and Regulatory) Bill 2007, when cleared, might take care of the problem. But the issue does not brook any further delay. More importantly, the present macroeconomic policy mix which supports the MFIs in their new avatar does not make any economic sense. Why should public sector banks support commercial MFIs? This need to be rectified and the focus should be on the development the home-grown micro finance segment. The Commercial MFIs seek to take shelter under the umbrella of financial inclusion and this raises the whole host of basic issues of our approach to financial inclusion. This address attempts to demonstrate that the present approach to financial inclusion is flawed: we cannot reduce the exercise to a game of numbers. Thus, this address seeks to provide inputs for introspection on these macroeconomic policy issues relating to future development of the micro finance sector.

Official Blessings: Interest Rates

What is disturbing is that such exorbitant interest rates charged by MFIs have the official blessings. First, let us have a look at the rates:

Table 2.1: Interest Charges by Micro Finance Institutions (March 2006)

(Per cent)

State (1)	Range of Cost to the Borrower (2)
Andhra Pradesh	17.0 to 32.5
Karnataka	12.0 to 40.0
Orissa	14.0 to 24.5
Rajasthan	16.0
Uttar Pradesh	13.0 to 26.0

Source: Report on Costs and Margins of Micro Finance Institutions, College of Agricultural Banking, Reserve Bank of India, Pune, January 2007.

On these rates, the Report of the Working Group on Benchmark Primary Lending Rate had these comments to offer........ "there are no restrictions on lending rates of micro-finance institutions (MFIs). The experiences of several successful Self-help Groups (SHGs) in India suggest that they charge relatively higher interest rates on loans to beneficiaries. Despite charging higher interest rates, MFIs are able to keep their delinquencies at low levels. Besides successful cross-country experiences in micro and rural credit also underline that timely availability of credit is more important, than the cost of credit".[4]

This is a dangerous argument. If this were true, then moneylenders would have developed rural India long, long ago, because they were more easily accessible to poor borrowers than the present-day MFIs. Our policy makers must realise that access to "affordable credit", or banking services in general, is the *sine qua non* of inclusive growth with equity.

The track record of financial sector reforms in India clearly demonstrates that the reformers have not covered themselves in glory. Those who pontificate on why concessional lending rates do not help the poor, further expose their innocence of the realities of the present interest rate structure. Financial and banking sector reforms introduced in the 1990s resulted in the emergence of an inequitable interest rate structure: a structure designed to pamper the private corporate sector, and which is biased against agricultural sector and the small borrowers generally. For instance, a small farmer was made to pay an interest rate of 12 per cent at a time when a highly rated corporate entity could raise money from banks at 6 per cent. This paradoxical situation was the result of mindless implementation of Basel norms and adoption, without adaptation, of concepts like "risks" as understood in the developed world. As I have discussed elsewhere, this concept of risk should be made to stand on its head.[5] When some of us raised this uncomfortable question of inequitable interest rate structure in the early 1990s, the Reserve Bank of India (RBI) ignored the protest.[6] Wisdom finally dawned on RBI in 2005-06, when its Report on Currency and Finance admitted: "to compensate for such sub-BPLR lending, other segments are charged higher rates of interest, leading "to cross subsidisation of the economically well-off borrowers by the economically poor borrowers".[7] This is indeed disturbing especially when the objective both of inclusive growth in the real sector and financial inclusion is to promote growth with equity. It is to the credit of RBI that they eventually brought out the problem in the open and appointed a Working Group in April 2008 to look into the issue. The Working Group on Benchmark Prime Lending Rate submitted its Report in October 2009. As a result of the Group's recommendation, the banking system switched over from Benchmark Prime Lending Rate to the Base Rate System with effect from July 1, 2010. The Base Rates set by major banks are in the range of 7.25 per cent to 8 per cent. In retrospect, we can see how the previous interest rate regime "exploited" the small borrowers, including the small farmers, by charging, say, 12 per cent. While the corporate sector is quite vocal in seeking a low interest rate regime for itself, on the pretext that high interest rates would adversely affect growth, the policy makers were insensitive to unmerited interest rate burden inflicted on the silent, small borrowers. It took almost two decades, for the RBI to correct the distortion in the interest rate structure.

New Avatar of MFIs

The recent faster growth of MFIs clearly shows that they have metamorphosed into glorified moneylenders, charging exorbitant interest rates of 30 or 40 per cent. This is further corroborated by the fact that engagement of MFIs with borrowers has been shallow based on "touch and move on" business models, shorn of any development content. "The average loans per client in both MFIs and SHGs have been low: between Rs. 3,500 and Rs. 5,000. The duration of the loan is short, typically one year or less. The small loan size and short duration do not enable most borrowers to do much except to ease liquidity problems".[8] Furthermore, investigative researchers have thrown up some evidence which indicates that MFIs are leveraging public funds for generating private profits. Some case studies show how the families acquired significant holding in the MFI concerned through an irregular mechanism and the remuneration packages to one Managing Director of an MFI was more than Rs. 8 crore and in another case a total of Rs. 3.5 crore.[9] Are the poor borrowers squeezed to facilitate personal enrichment of the promoters or management of the MFIs? Of course, profits as such are not to be shunned, because they are essential for sustainability and growth of the institution. What is abhorred is profiteering, especially by an institution with pretensions to help the poor.

In this context, one is reminded of the interesting statement of President Barack Obama made recently at a correspondents' Dinner:

"All of the jokes here tonight are brought to you by Goldman Sachs. So you don't have to worry—they make money whether you laugh or not".

Public Sector Support

If MFIs made rapid progress during more recent years, it is in no small measure due to not only "official blessings" to which I referred earlier, but also due to active public sector support. Such support is available from public sector banks (PSBs) NABARD and SIDBI; and of course, from RBI. For instance, during 2008-09 banks extended loans to 581 MFIs amounting to Rs. 3,732 crore, taking the total amount of outstanding loans to Rs. 5009 crore, at the end of March 2009. Such support is perhaps justifiable if the beneficiary MFIs belong to "not for profits" category. If such MFIs borrow at say 13 or 14 per cent from banks and onlend at 15 or 16 per cent, it is perfectly understandable. If commercial MFIs begin to onlend at 30 per cent, what they have borrowed at 13 per cent from PSBs, are we not assisting profiteering by Commercial MFIs? It is important to ensure that resources of PSBs are not used to perpetuate usurious lending practices of commercial MFIs. Similarly, NABARD is using its Micro Finance Development and Equity Fund (MFDEF) to support a variety of interventions like providing quasi-equity support to MFIs. Strange enough, NABARD Chairman, is fully aware of the exploitative character of commercial MFIs: "Some of the practices that are followed by certain MFIs do not seem to be appropriate. The lack of transparency, the ill-designed products, inadequate communication with clients and unfriendly methods of recovery are not consistent with the objectives of serving the poor".[10]

The simple course that NABARD could have taken is not to support such commercial MFIs.

Now take SIDBI: “SIDBI has, over the past seven years, made multifarious efforts to develop the MFI sector. These have, no doubt, yielded good results, but still much more needs to be done to enable the micro finance sector to increase its outreach and scale as a step to access financial inclusion.”[11] SIDBI has been providing a comprehensive package of services like capacity building, equity and term loans, to ensure holistic growth of MFI sector. It has been making equity investment through SIDBI Growth Fund of Rs. 50 crore. But one of the important recommendations of its Report is: “MFIs should follow a rational and transparent interest rate policy to avoid suspicious and encourage professionalism in the sector”.

It is quite obvious that RBI has no clear vision of how the MFI sector should be made to grow. Why should PSBs, NABARD and SIDBI be permitted to support commercial MFIs which are exploitative — in the nature of these glorified moneylenders? Public sector institutions should have been, from the beginning, more discriminatory by supporting only "not-for profit" MFIs.

Financial Inclusion

The only excuse for supporting even commercial MFIs is that the rapid progress of MFIs in recent years has raised high expectations about the role they can play in financial inclusion. Our submission is that RBI's approach to financial inclusion in the sense of universal or 100 per cent coverage of households is basically misconceived. Banking sector resources are, and would continue to be, limited. Optimum utilisation of banking sector resources would demand a selective approach to credit extension. Ideally, credit should follow productive activities and universal coverage would be tantamount to de-hyphenating credit and productive activities: this does not augur well for facilitating inclusive growth in the real sector. If credit is made to chase productive activities, we would promote optimal use of banking sector resources. Spreading available resources too thinly, which universal coverage necessarily implies, would not serve to optimize growth.

Today, financial inclusion has been reduced to a game of numbers, a mere tokenism. Take for instance, “No Frills Accounts” which banks are required to open with very low or even “nil” balances. Since November 2005, about 33 million accounts have been opened but as Dr. Tarapore points out, only a tenth of these accounts are operational. Such target fixation could be counterproductive.[12] What purpose on earth such “near-dead” accounts serve? Only RBI could provide an answer to this question. The whole approach to universal financial coverage thus appears flawed and hence RBI needs to take a second look at it.

In any case, one thing is quite clear. Let us not commit a serious mistake by allowing these glorified moneylenders to flourish in the name of financial inclusion.

Concluding Comments

If the future growth of the micro finance sector is viewed in this proper perspective, the changes warranted in the macroeconomic policy mix become clear. Basically, a more meaningful approach to financial inclusion needs to be adopted. It should cease to be a numbers' game. Target fixing and pressurizing PSBs to reach them has proved to be counterproductive. Credit, and affordable credit, must chase productive activities.

In the final analysis, the home-grown segment of the micro finance sector holds out great promise for financial inclusion because this segment has succeeded in blending "for profit" and social banking. In fact, historically, it was the father of nationalization of commercial banks in 1969 who heralded financial inclusion movement much before financial inclusion became fashionable in the international financial lexicon. The phenomenal bank branches expansion in the post-nationalization phase was unprecedented in the history of world banking.

The "for-profit" or only "for-profit" MFIs should have no place in our financial inclusion programme, since they represent the predatory face of financial capitalism. It is not enough to place a ceiling on their lending rates. Also, public sector institutions should be more discriminatory in extending their assistance which should be restricted to "Not for Profit" MFIs.

In any case, the home-grown segment of micro finance is already expanding its universe of borrowers by innovative methods. PSBs have adopted a system of multichannel delivery of credit. In particular, the business correspondent (BC) model seems to be catching on. The outreach of PSBs is being extended not only through brick and mortar branches but also through correspondents. On the other hand, following the recommendations of the Prime Minister's Task Force on Micro, Small and Medium Enterprises (MSMEs), the RBI has recently asked banks to: (i) achieve a 20 per cent year-on-year growth in credit to micro and small enterprises; (ii) achieve an allocation of 60 per cent of MSE advances to micro enterprises by 2012-13; and (iii) achieve 10 per cent annual growth in the number of micro enterprise accounts.[13]

Recapitalization and amalgamation of Regional Rural Banks (RRBs) has injected an element of dynamism into them. Out of the total of 86, the number of profit making RRBs increased to 80 in March 2009. Productivity of RRBs, both in terms per branch and per employee has been improving consistently during the last few years. Surprisingly, the RRB making the highest profit comes from Bihar: the Uttar Bihar Gramin Bank made net profit of Rs. 104 crore in 2009.[14] We may even think of replicating these successful models in other areas. The prospects of converting the network of Post Offices into a vibrant channel of credit delivery are quite bright.

The main point to drive home is that the growth of micro finance sector could be supported by the home-grown micro finance segment, if appropriate changes are introduced in the macroeconomic policy mix. India does not have to face the dilemma of sacrificing social banking to be able to achieve such growth.

Wisdom seems to be dawning on the RBI, at last. Last month, RBI made appropriate noises about why PSBs should support "for-profit" MFIs. The real question is: why, in the first place, PSBs were allowed, if not encouraged, to lend to such MFIs, without stipulating a ceiling on their onlending rates? Secondly, in its Annual Report for 2009-10, RBI states: "On balance, ensuring credit at affordable prices and furthering financial inclusion are cherished objectives" (p. 95, emphasis supplied). This is a complete reversal of RBI's earlier stand, to which I referred. I only hope that RBI will not take another decade to implement the correctives to distortions in the macroeconomic policy mix and the interest rate policy.

This is the edited version of the Keynote Address delivered on September 24, 2010, at the National Seminar on "Rethinking on Micro Finance in the Current Scenario" organised by the Oriental Institute of Management, Mumbai.

References

1. Preface to the Report: Micro Finance, *Banana Skins*, 2009, CSFI, New York, June 2009.
2. The recent success of IPO of SKS Micro finance is a case in point. It attracted high profile investors like billionaire George Soros, venture capitalists, Vinod Khosla and Infosys founder Narayan Murthy, *Economic Times*, 4th August, 2010.
3. Assessing Development Impact of Micro Finance Programmes, SIDBI, Lucknow, September 2008.
4. Report of the Working Group on Benchmark Prime Lending Rate (Chairman: Deepak Mohanty), Reserve Bank of India, Mumbai, 2009-10.
5. Risk, Uncertainties, and Rural Credit in Indian Agriculture, included in the book: *Inclusive Growth*, Academic Foundation, New Delhi, 2007.

6. *Financial Sector Reforms and India's Economic Development*, N.A. Mujumdar, Academic Foundation, New Delhi, 2002, (2 Volumes).

7. *Report on Currency and Finance 2005-06*, Reserve Bank of India, Mumbai, (p. 159).

8. *Micro Finance India: State of the Sector Report 2008*, Sage Publications, New Delhi, India, 2008, p. 3.

9. Commercialisation of Micro Finance in India, A Discussion of the Emperor's Apparel, M.S. Sriram, *Economic and Political Weekly*, June 12-18, 2010, p.15.

10. Interview of Shri U.C. Sarangi, Chairman, NABARD with Shri N. Srinivasan, See Report cited in (8) above, p. 37.

11. See the Report cited in (3) above page.

12. *Configuration of the Banking System in the Next Decade*, Dr. S.S. Tarapore, Address at the Dun and Bradstreet — Polar is Software Event, Mumbai, on August 18, 2010.

13. See *Monetary and Credit Information Review*, July 2010, RBI, Mumbai.

14. *Gramin Banks Bounce Back*, Dr. N.K. Thingalaya, 2010.

3

SHF – Bank Linkage Programme: Practices and Lessons for Future

Dr. S.L. Kumbhare[1]
CGM, MCID, NABARD

Introduction

The nature and extent of financial exclusion[i] of poor from the purview of formal credit delivery system suggested the need for new products and delivery mechanisms which could bring down the transaction costs both for borrowers and lenders and offer the poor an affordable way of getting financial services from banks (Bakshi, 2010). This *inter alia* led to SHG-Bank Linkage Programme (SHG-BLP) by NABARD which was the supplementary and not necessarily the alternative credit delivery mechanism. The focus was on savings first followed by credit. The programme as spelt out later indicated its success in quantitative term *inter alia* due to policy support from Reserve Bank of India (RBI) and the Government of India.

The SHGs are informal associations of less than 20 persons, who are homogeneous in terms of social and economic status. These affinity groups come together voluntarily to save regularly, undertake regular meetings, undertake internal lending, regularly repay the loans taken and regularly maintain the books relating to transactions and decisions taken in the meetings. These five aspects

---

1. The author is working in National Bank for Agriculture and Rural Development, NABARD, Mumbai. The views expressed in this paper are of the author and not of the institution to which he belongs.

i. Lack of access to basic financial products and services offered by mainstream financial institutions in a fair, transparent and cost-effective manner. This is based on a talk delivered at College of Agricultural Banking (RBI), Pune by Dr. K.C. Chakravarty, Dy. Governor, Reserve Bank of India. The talk was delivered on 24th April, 2010.

ultimately decide the quality and sustenance of the SHGs. The objective of the programme is to ensure that every member of the group becomes independent client of the formal banking system.

The SHG-BLP launched by NABARD in 1992[ii] as a pilot project was aimed at testing the hypothesis that, the poor are bankable. The pilot project proved that poor can save and has now become a movement throughout the country. As on 31st March, 2009, there are more than 61 lakh savings-linked SHGs and about 42 lakh credit-linked SHGs and thus, about 8.6 crore poor households are covered under the programme (Table 3.1). However, the issue of regional imbalance, quality of SHGs, micro enterprise promotion among SHG members, recovery performance, etc., need to be addressed with much more determination for orderly growth of micro finance movement.

Against this background, the paper examines: (a) the outreach of SHG-BLP, (b) Quality of SHGs, (c) Regional spread of SHG-BLP, (d) Graduation of SHG members to Micro Enterprises, and (e) Recovery/Non-performing Assets (NPAs) under the programme, etc. (Sections II through VI). The lessons for SHG-BLP for the future are also addressed in concerned sections of this paper. The discussion is limited to SHGs in rural areas[iii].

SHG-Bank Linkage Programme — Widening and Deepening

An analysis of progress of the SHG-BLP over 18 years (Table 1) shows that, promotion of initial one lakh SHGs and their credit linkage with banks took eight years. However, in a span of another four years, the programme achieved milestone of more than one million SHGs and their linkage with the banks. The success in terms of number of SHGs and their linkage with banks could be attributed to efforts of Self-help Group promoting institutions, viz., Non-government Organizations,[iv] Banks themselves, especially RRB and co-operatives, policy support of Reserve Bank of India, grant support of NABARD for training, etc.

ii. Since 1984, affinity-based groups emerged in Mysore Resettlement and Development Agency (MYRADA) and were called credit management groups. When MYRADA collaborated with NABARD in 1986-87, to commission a pilot project to promote these groups, the name was changed from Credit Management Group to Self-help Group (SHG).

iii. The rural areas where population is less than **50,0000.**

iv. Two-thirds of groups are promoted and linked to banks by NGOs.

Table 3.1: Progress of SHG-Bank Linkage Programme

Year	*No. of SHGs Credit Linked (Cumulative)*	*Bank Loan Outstanding (Rs. Crore)*	*No. of Persons Trained through Grant Support of NABARD*
1992-93	255	0.29	
1993-94	620	0.65	
1994-95	2,112	2.44	
1995-96	4,757	6.06	
1996-98	8,598	11.84	
1998-99	14,317	23.76	
1999-00	32,995	57.07	43069
2000-01	**1,14,775**	**192.87**	**171638**
2001-02	2,63,825	480.87	89698
2002-03	4,61,478	1026.3	194817
2003-04	**7,17,360**	**2048.68**	**244000**
2004-05	10,79,091	3904.2	3299943
2005-06	16,18,456	6898.46	283531
2006-07	**28,94,505**	12366.49	272773
2007-08	36,25,941	16999.91	371398
2008-09	42,24,338	22679.84	283998

Source: Various issues of *'Status of Micro Finance in India'* published by MCID, NABARD.

The three decisions taken by the Reserve bank of India, and followed by NABARD, can be considered as important steps in the SHG-BLP. These steps were: (a) Allowing the banks to lend to unregistered SHGs, provided they saved, maintained records of decisions and accounts, (b) Allowing the banks to lend to SHGs without asking for the purpose prior to lending and (c) Lending to SHGs without physical collateral provided there was adequate social capital — an affinity based on mutual trust, backed up by the habit of savings and at least six months experience of internal lending.

Besides, the SHG-BLP also received support from the Government of India in terms of policy pronouncements. In Union Budget of 2000-01, the Government of India announced the establishment of Micro Finance Development Fund (MFDF) with a corpus of Rs.100 crore with an objective to up-scale the quality and depth of micro finance interventions in the country. The Fund was then redesignated as Micro Finance Development and Equity Fund (MFDEF) and the corpus augmented to Rs.200 crore, as per the Union Budget for 2005-06 with additional focus of providing capital to MFIs for leveraging funds so as to enable the poor to have access to financial services at affordable costs. In 2006-07, Budget announcements specified that banks will open separate window for SHGs/JLGs of farmers and NABARD would open separate line of credit for financing farm production and investment activities through the SHG route (NABARD, 2006). In the Union Budget of 2009-10, it was stated that the objective of SHG programme is to enroll at least 50 per cent of all rural women in India as members of SHGs over next five years and link these SHGs to Banks. Hon'ble Union Finance Minister in his budget speech on 26th February 2010, announced that, the corpus of Micro Finance Development and Equity Fund (MFDEF) would be doubled to Rs. 400 crore from the existing Rs. 200 crore since 2005-06.

The growth in SHG-BLP was *inter alia* set in motion by the grant support extended by NABARD to various partner agencies like NGOs, banks, PRIs, anganwadi workers, and individuals. Grant support extended by NABARD in terms of number of partners and amount has increased over the years but proportion of SHGs supported by NABARD though grant support is around 6 per cent only and thus NABARD's support was only catalytic in nature. As on 31st March, 2010, NABARD has extended support to 2,911 partners, involving grant support of Rs. 40.4 crore and credit linking of 2.37 lakh SHGs♦ with banks. Growth in SHG-BLP with an improved savings and loan disbursement possibly shows success of market-led solution for financial services.

Major challenge in SHG-BLP is to cover 144 million rural households (BCG, 2010) as only 37 per cent of the total 88,000 branches are in rural areas and 60 per cent of the population does not have bank accounts (*Financial Express*, 15th August, 2010). Between 2000 and 2009, the proportion of rural branches decreased by 1.2 per cent (BCG, 2010) and we may have to look for local institutions and their members for promotion of SHGs wherever, NGOs are not readily available. Members of matured SHGs could be used for promotion of the SHGs. The linkage of these SHGs, among

---

♦ Some of the NGOs are associated with Watershed development, Tribal development, Entrepreneurship development and promotion of SHGs in their area of operation.

other things also depends upon the attitude of bank branch officials. Some of these issues call for regular training of bank officials and others involved in the programme as it will have an impact on quality of SHGs also. **Capacity building of stakeholders could be addressed through public investment or banks can arrange it as it has an impact on quality of SHGs and ultimately the loan portfolio.**

Quality of SHGs under SHG-Bank Linkage Programme

Quality of SHGs can be examined in terms of five basic parameters of SHG functioning, viz., regularity in savings, meetings, internal lending, repayments and maintenance of books. Alternatively, average loans size of SHGs can indicate quality. Average loan disbursed per SHG between 2005-06 and 2008-09 was Rs. 72,552, Rs. 59,420, Rs. 72,076, and Rs. 76128. During 2006-07, the average loan size was Rs. 59,420 mainly due to change in the MIS data collection format. **During the remaining years, the average loan size of the SHGs hovered around Rs. 72,000 showing a marginal increase in 2008-09. This stagnation in loan size can be read as a sign of unsatisfactory quality of SHGs as the banker seems averse to taking the risk of higher financing.**

A study by APMAS found that 40 per cent of the SHGs were of inadequate quality to access bank linkage (Shylendra, 2006). Limited field experience in Rajasthan suggested that 30 per cent of SHGs were of 'A' grade quality in terms of regular meetings, savings, bookkeeping, attendance in meetings, rotation of leadership, etc.

A study by Sa-Dhan[4] (an association of MFIs in India) on quality of SHGs indicates that the: (a) SHGs promoted by Self-help Promoting Institutions (SHPIs) registered as Society/Trust, as legal constitution, were of better quality, (b) SHGs functioning in southern and northern regions were of better quality than SHGs in eastern and western regions, (c) Almost no SHG obtained good grading in terms of performance in social and community action and (d) SHGs older than 24 months did not exhibit all the qualities of matured groups.[©]

Significant financial investment, capacity building and technical support are required for meeting this challenge. NABARD has taken up various measures like barefoot accountant, computer 'munshi', smart card and Individual Rural Volunteer

© The details of matured SHGs have not been spelt out but some of these as per our experience could be rotation of leadership, internal lending, peer pressure for timely recovery of loan, social activities etc.

programmes (IRV) to combat this challenge. The IRV scheme is taken up with a view to finding solutions for the NGO deficit areas, where motivated and suitably oriented individuals can assume the NGO's role as well as handholding of the SHGs. Adequate resources for training and capacity building, avoidance of target-based approach and improved experience of promoting agencies may help in improving SHG's quality (Shylendra, 2006).

Adequacy of grant support from NABARD to an NGO for SHG-Bank Linkage and its relation with quality can be debated. We have to remember that the NGOs are possibly associated with social business wherein they are free from the pressure of earning profit for the owners. The organizations undertake SHG-BLP as "Add on activity" and need not have to assure certain minimum level of return on investment before they invest or create jobs (Yunus, M., 2009).

Regional Spread of SHG-BLP

There is a need for even distribution of group formation and linkage efforts especially in the Northern, Central, Eastern and North-Eastern States to put a check on high concentration and uneven spread of the SHG-Bank Linkage Programme in the Southern region (54%) of the country (Table 3.2). This is important in view of higher concentration of the rural poor in other regions.

Table 3.2: Growth in SHG-Bank Linkage Programme — Inequalities across Regions

Particulars	2005	2006	2007	2008	2009
No. of SHGs credit linked to Banks (lakh) @	16.18	22.38	29.25	36.26	41.45
Share of Southern region	58	54	52	51	55

@ Cumulative till 2007 and Loan Outstanding Accounts from 2008 onwards

Source: Srinivasan, *op. cit.*

As indicated elsewhere, there is a need to invest much more in capacity building programmes in these areas. NABARD has been giving greater thrust for upscaling the SHG-BLP in 13 priority states (Himachal Pradesh, Rajasthan, Assam, Bihar, Jharkhand, Orissa, West Bengal, Chattisgarh, Madhya Pradesh, Uttarakhand, Uttar Pradesh, Gujarat, and Maharashtra) within these regions. The share of credit linked SHGs in priority states increased over a period of time. Quick available estimates for priority states indicates that the number of SHGs during 2008-09 were 5.22 lakh whereas the number increased to 5.72 lakh during 2009-10.

Micro Finance to Livelihood

A Study on 'Impact and Sustainability of SHG-Bank Linkage Programme' was conducted by the National Council of Applied Economic Research (NCAER). The study was conducted to assess the impact and sustainability of SHG-Bank Linkage on the socio-economic conditions of the individual members and their households in the pre-SHG and post-SHG scenarios. The study was conducted in six States (Andhra Pradesh, Karnataka, Maharashtra, Orissa, Uttar Pradesh and Assam) from five regions, viz., the South, West, East, Central and North-east. The overall findings of the study suggest that SHG-BLP had significantly improved the access to financial services by the rural poor.

The graduation of SHG members from "borrowing for consumption" stage to borrowing for starting or supporting livelihood is a natural progression in the credit profile of the SHG members. An impact evaluation study (NABARD, 2007) conducted during 2006-07, covering 310 members from 56 matured SHGs (which were at least three years old) in Chittoor, Nizamabad and Warangal districts of Andhra Pradesh revealed that 70 per cent of the members had initiated or supported Income Generating Activities (IGA) but only 28 per cent of them had ventured into micro enterprises (MEs; An ME implied an IGA by creation of an asset with or without credit support). These enterprises were standalone or family-owned MEs like dairy, pickle preparation, flourmill, grocery, etc. Average loan amount availed by members with MEs and IGAs was Rs. 24,089 and Rs. 17,171 respectively. The net income accrued and the employment generated through the ME households were higher by 70 per cent and 81 per cent respectively as compared to non-IGA households who availed the average loan of Rs. 8,210 only.

In Gujarat, the percentage of bank loans utilized in asset creation improved from 8 per cent in the first linkage to 67 per cent by the fifth linkage. The percentage of members graduating to micro enterprises (dairy, flour mill, rickshaw, grocery shop, brick kiln, mandap decoration, etc.) varied between 29 per cent in Gujarat and 32 per cent in Jammu & Kashmir. IGA households undertook purchase of inputs for farm enterprises, mushroom cultivation, etc., and the proportion of such members was 35 per cent and 39 per cent among the members in Gujarat and Jammu & Kashmir, respectively (Table 3.3). Improvement in livelihood creation through micro finance calls for provision of micro finance plus by banks or banks can arrange the same suitable agencies. Further, field experience has shown that six to eight or some times even more cycles of credit are required for a family to realize an adequate income. While arranging training, family could be considered rather than one member of the family as enterprises with micro finance are family operated and not the individual-centric.

Table 3.3: Micro Enterprises among SHG Members[2]

State	No. of SHG Members Studied	% of SHG Members Undertaking		Recovery %
		Income Generating Activities	Micro-Enterprises @	
Gujarat	49	35	29	93
Jammu & Kashmir	150	39	32	100
Andhra Pradesh	310	70	28	94

@ Micro enterprise is an income generating activity by creating an asset with/without credit support.

Source: Annual Reports of NABARD (2006-07 and 2008-09)

Recovery/Non-performing Assets

In certain quarters, it is viewed that growth of SHG-BLP with inadequate attention to quality of groups is leading to rising overdues/non-performing assets. On the basis of data reported by banks, 181 out of 267 banks (67.8%) had more than 80 per cent recovery of SHG loans as on 31st March, 2009, which was observed to be the same as on 31st March, 2008. As regards recovery percentage of SHG loans under SGSY, out of total 185 banks reported, 109 banks (58.9%) had more than 80 per cent recovery of SHG loans as on 31st March, 2009 as against 55.3 per cent, as on 31st March, 2008.

As on 31st March, 2009, Non-performing Assets to total bank loans outstanding against SHGs were 2.9 per cent as against 5 per cent in case of SHGs under SGSY. **Literature also indicates that repayment rates for business loans are strikingly lower, than the average and this relative difficulty in repaying loans may be one**

2. In Gujarat and Jammu & Kashmir, absence of rotation in leadership, declining membership of SHG over time, lack of product diversification, use of low level technology, inadequate infrastructure, etc., were some of the constraints identified in promotion of MEs. While in Andhra Pradesh, absence of strong support system for supply of raw material, technology upgradation, capacity building of entrepreneurs and marketing arrangements were the major constraints.

of the reasons for lesser evidence of enterprise development among weaker sections (Jones, P.). Extent of recovery at borrower level/group level needs to be documented as it will indicate the sustainability of groups.

Conclusion

Savings led Credit Programme captioned as SHG-Bank Linkage Programme has completed eighteen years and during this period the lessons learnt included: (i) poor can save on regular basis and savings can help them as risk mitigating strategy, (ii) existing stakeholders like banks and civil society organizations could be used for promoting and linking of SHGs with the banks, (iii) lending through banks can have linkage with savings but change in attitude of banks is essential to follow progressive lending and savings to loan ratio can be raised up to 1:10, (iv) capacity building of stakeholders needs to be ensured through public investments, (v) banks also need to ensure training and awareness creation exercises through their training institutes in view of the business potential of SHGs, (vi) market-based solution to financial access to poor has *inter alia* succeeded due to initiatives of apex financial institutions and policy pronouncements. The latter included, allowing the banks to lend to informal groups without asking for purpose of loan and collateral except social capital.

Regional inequalities, quality of SHGs and graduation from SHGs to micro enterprises are important areas of concern and could be addressed through Banking Facilitators (BFs)/Correspondents (BCs) after initial handholding by SHG promoting institutions. Banks can consider the remuneration to BFs/BCs, as the banks earn interest income through lending to SHGs. The issue of recovery at group and individual level need to be examined to ascertain extent of sustainability of groups although at bank level, non-performing assets under SHG-BLP are around three per cent and is an area of concern.

Matured SHGs can be facilitated to carry out the wide spectrum of value chain in farm and non-farm sectors through establishment of forward/backward linkages. In addition, matured SHGs are likely to assume the role of Business Facilitators and Business Correspondents. Wherever feasible, banks may provide or arrange for credit plus approach while purveying micro finance. ICT solutions need to be used extensively by banks to reduce transaction costs and compete with Micro Financial Institutions which are increasing their business at faster pace. Banks may feel comfortable today because they can meet their priority sector targets by financing

MFIs. However, the next phase of development in terms of market for consumer goods has to be rural India and the banks may miss out on that opportunity as MFIs would take over the same. Continued dependence on civil societies need to be reduced through promotion of SHG Federations undertaking primarily non-financial intermediation.

References

1. Bakshi, P. (2010), "Promoting Agricultural Development in India, NABARD — An Interview", News and Views, WSBI, June 2010, pp. 27-28.
2. Boston Consultancy Group, Federation of Indian Chambers of Commerce and Indian Bank Association (2010), "Indian Banking 2020 Making the Decade's Promise Come True", p. 18.
3. Fernandez, Aloysius Prakash (2006), "Sustainability of Self-help Affinity Groups or SHGs as understood by MYRADA", *Towards Sustainable Micro Finance Outreach in India*, Book Published by NABARD, GTZ and SDC, pp. 83-102.
4. Jones, J.H.M. (2006), "Some Issues in Informal Finance Perspectives from a Rajasthan Village", *Towards a Sustainable Micro Finance Outreach in India: Experience and Perspectives*, pp. 137-152.
5. Karmakar, K.G. (2009), "Micro Finance Revisited", *Micro Finance in India*, (Ed.) K.G. Karmakar, Sage Publication, pp. 33-54.
6. Kumbhare, S.L. and Darad, R. (2010), "Livelihood through SHG", *Micro Finance World*, April-June, pp. 10-13.
7. NABARD (1995), "Study of Credit Management Groups", Department of Economic Analysis and Research, Mumbai, p. 8.
8. NABARD (2006), "Annual Report – 2005-06", p. 25.
9. NABARD (2007), "Annual Report – 2006-07", p. 25.
10. NABARD (2009), "Annual Report – 2008-09", p. 40.
11. Premchander, S. and Chidambaranathan, (2007), "One Step Forward or Two Steps Back?", *Economic and Political Weekly*, Vol. XLII, No.12, March 24-30, pp. 1006-1008.

12. Rangarajan, C. (2006), "Micro Finance and Its Future Directions", *Towards a Sustainable Micro Finance Outreach in India — Experience and Perspectives, op. cit.*, pp. 19-26.

13. Sa-Dhan (2009), The Bharat Micro Finance Report — Responsive Growth Side by Side, p. 30.

14. Samrani, S. (1982), "Rapporteur's Report on Subsidy is Instrument for Increasing Agricultural Production and Income", *Indian Journal of Agricultural Economics*, July-September.

15. Shylendra, H.S. (2006), "Mainstreaming Micro Finance for Poverty Alleviation — Need for a Proactive Pricing and Regulatory Framework", *Towards a Sustainable Micro Finance Outreach in India, op. cit.*, pp. 175-185.

16. Srinivasan, N. (2009), "Micro Finance India — State of the Sector Report 2009", Sage Publication, p. 23.

17. Thorat, Y.S.P. (2006), "Micro Finance in India — Sectoral Issues and Changes", *Towards a Sustainable Micro Finance Outreach in India — Experience and Perspectives*, pp. 23-40.

18. Tiwari, M. (2010), "Didi of Rural Bihar: Real Agent of Change", *Economic and Political Weekly*, XIV (33), pp. 27-30.

19. Yunus, M. (2009), "Social Business — A Step towards Creating a New Economic and Social Order", Second Annual Professor Hiren Mukerjee Parliamentary Memorial Lecture at Delhi, December 9, p. 15.

4

Micro Finance in India: Past, Present and Future*

Miss. Nidhi Chandra and Dr. R.K. Pattnaik,
Senior Professor, SIMSR

Abstract

In this paper, an attempt is made for assessing the impact of poverty and the role of micro finance in poverty alleviation. Poverty is exacerbated by further lack of financial services. Well developed and inclusive financial systems often lead to rapid economic development. Micro finance has been associated with poverty alleviation and is typically viewed as an economic development strategy. However, it is not a panacea for poverty reduction. Micro financing aims to alleviate poverty by stimulating economic growth through entrepreneurial initiative. But for this effort to be successful, it should be known to the people to whom it is offered, that how to utilize it. Therefore, financial inclusion efforts have to be complemented with initiatives of skill development, and provision of avenues to utilize the income generated in constructive manner. This requires an active participation of both governments and the NGOs.

Poverty and Its Impacts

Poverty is not only about having a very low income generation; instead it also covers other related aspects of low education, poor health and under nourishment, lack of basic hygiene, etc. All these, when coupled with low income generation, triggers a chain reaction which further increases poverty (Desta, Rafeal, 2009). It leads to lesser access to goods and services. Top 20% of the people in the world consume about 86% of the goods and services produced in the world (Gibson 2009).

Also, people with low income tend to reduce their children's time allotted to education when they either face negative income shock or when they face the risk of negative income shock, i.e., loss of employment, death in the family of the earning member, or loss of income due to any natural calamities, etc. In the latter case, even if the risk does not materialize, the children are deprived of education (Kazianga, 2005). Poverty can even lead to increased child labour. From the household's point of view, child labor entails a trade-off between immediate benefits (increased current income) and the future earning potential of the child (Beegle, Dehejia, Gatti, 2003). The family size of the extremely poor, defined as those living on less than $1 per day, also tends to be relatively large. The number of family members varies between about 6 and about 12, with a median value (across the different countries) of between 7 and 8, compared to 2.5 in the 2000 US census. A large family size, with low income levels, lead to health problems, like malnutrition, low body mass index (BMI), anemia, poor vision and the like (Banerjee and Duflo, 2006).

Poverty has an impact on the earning habits of the people as well. All over the world, a substantial fraction of the poor act as entrepreneurs in the sense of raising the capital, carrying out the investment, and being the full residual claimants for the earnings. Even those who are not entrepreneurs, seek out earning opportunities at different avenues, so as not to become specialized. There are two main reasons for it. First, spreading of risk, so that going away of one of the options does not impair their earning capability much and they have other earning avenues open for them. Second, many a times they even do not have the funds to run a task that would fully employ them (Banerjee and Duflo, 2006).

Financial Inclusion and Poverty

Poverty is exacerbated by further lack of financial services. The low income group is denied credit access by the formal financial markets because of their poor credit worthiness, lack of collaterals, not verifiable credit history. This forces them to approach the non-formal financial markets, which provide credit facilities at exorbitantly high interest rates (Desta, Rafeal, 2009).

According to the research, well developed and inclusive financial systems often lead to rapid economic development and reduction of income inequalities. It helps the poor catch up with the rest of the economy as it grows (Basu Priya, 2005).

Financial Inclusion is delivery of banking services at an affordable cost to the vast sections of disadvantaged and low income groups. Unrestrained access to public goods and services is the *sine qua non* of an open and efficient society. As banking services are in the nature of public good, it is essential that availability of banking and payment services to the entire population without discrimination is the prime objective of the public policy (V. Leeladhar, 2005).

The UN identifies four pillars to inclusive finance as: (1) a sound policy, (2) regulatory and legal framework, (3) sound financial institutions and (4) various products and services catering to the needs of the people. However, these pillars alone cannot help in achieving full extent of inclusion, other considerations like the degree of financial literacy and the degree to which right to fair treatment of the individual in the society (UN Bluebook, 2005).

Micro finance is typically viewed as an economic development strategy, and it is a particularly relevant approach in countries where disadvantaged groups tend not to benefit from involvement in the formal economy (Doocy *et al.*, 2005). Apart from providing credit and saving facilities, it also provides facilities like insurance and mortgages, which are specifically designed for the people who were previously excluded from the formal means of borrowing and lending (Khavul, 2010). Thus, Micro finance has the potential of financial inclusion.

Definition of Micro Finance

The proposed Micro Finance Services Regulation Bill defines micro finance services as "providing financial assistance to an individual or an eligible client, either directly or through a group mechanism for:

(1) an amount, not exceeding rupees fifty thousand in aggregate per individual, for small and tiny enterprise, agriculture, allied activities (including for consumption purposes of such individual)

or

(2) an amount not exceeding rupees one lakh fifty thousand in aggregate per individual for housing purposes

or

(3) such other amounts, for any of the purposes mentioned at items (1) and (2) above or other purposes, as may be prescribed." (NABARD)

Micro Finance Origin in India

As stated earlier, well developed and inclusive financial systems often lead to rapid economic development and reduction of income inequalities (Basu Priya, 2005).

This was realized early in the independent India, and attempts of bringing financial inclusion was started in the 1950s itself. As majority of the low income population in India reside in villages, the policies had a rural focus. A large number of Rural Cooperative banks were set up. However, the attempt was not very effective. Therefore, nationalization of banks took place in 1969, so as to prevent a few corporations from controlling the banks and so that the savings of people could also be mobilized for the rural areas. This resulted in a massive branch expansion in the rural and semi-urban areas. Policies for priority sector lending were also in place for agriculture, small-scale industry, self-employed and small business sectors and weaker sections within these sectors. As a result, the branches of scheduled commercial banks increased from 8,262 in June 1969 to 69,471 in March 2006. The average population per branch office decreased significantly from 64,000 to 16,000 during the above period, with the share of rural branches increasing from 22.2 per cent in June 1969 to a little over 51 per cent in March 1998 (Priya Basu,2005, Thorat, 2007). Also, a 'Service Area Approach' was established, according to which one bank branch was allocated to a particular service area which generally ranged from 15-20 villages. Other banks which wanted to set up their branches in any of those areas, needed to get a 'No Objection' from the existing bank.

However, the post-liberalization period witnessed more number of private and foreign banks setting up in India, inducing greater competition among the banks, and pressure on the profit margins. By June 1993, 172 out of 196 Regional Rural Banks (RRBs) were unprofitable, despite their wide geographical coverage (Thorat, Bhatt, 2001).

In spite of the measures taken by the government, gaps remained in provision of financial services to the low income group. The public sector banks continuously fell short of their targets, though they were better than their private sector counterparts. The banks lending to weaker sections also had nigh NPA (Non-performing Assets) which affected their profitability. This led to the Non-governmental Organizations (NGOs) to come up with a micro finance sector (Sriram, M.S., 2003). The Micro Finance Institutions (MFIs) could play a significant role in financial inclusion owing largely to their reach, local know-how, and the needs of the people present in the geographical area where they operate (NABARD, 2008). This movement got a major boost in 1992, when the SHG-Bank Linkage Programme (SBLP) began, and was included in the targets of priority sector lending of banks.

Micro Finance Objective

The main objective of micro finance is economic development and improving the status of the low income group (Doocy *et al.*, 2005). Many researchers also believed that poverty alleviation can be achieved through micro credit. For example, it is stated in one of the research papers that Poverty is not only about having a very low income generation; instead it also covers other related aspects of low education, poor health and under nourishment, lack of basic hygiene, child labour, etc. All these, when coupled with low income generation, triggers a chain reaction which further increases poverty. This vicious cycle can be controlled and contained through micro finance services (Desta, Rafeal, 2009). The idea here is achieving Poverty alleviation through the mechanisms of Financial Inclusion.

The rationale behind Poverty Alleviation by extending financial services is as follows: Micro credit facilities when provided to the non-bankable without collaterals, it enables them to set up their own business and thus, be able to generate better and higher income for themselves. Similarly, micro savings helps in smoothing out any effect of the negative income shocks on the lives of the low income population (IMF, 2005).

A secondary objective of well-being of the low income group is also aimed. A small loan, a savings account or an insurance policy can make a great difference to a low income family. They enable people to invest in better nutrition, housing, health and education for their children (UN, 2006).

Activities contributing to well-being, like reduced child labour, and increased women empowerment can be important by-products of micro finance.

From the household's point of view, child labor entails a trade-off between immediate benefits (increased current income) and the future earning potential of the child (Beegle, Dehejia, Gatti, 2003). People with low income tend to reduce their children's time allotted to education when they either face negative income shock or when they face the risk of negative income shock, i.e., loss of employment, death in the family of the earning member, or droughts in the region, etc. In the latter case, even if the risk does not materialize, the children are deprived of education (Kazianga, 2005).

The prime beneficiaries of Micro finance movements in India have been women. Funds allotted for the various schemes like Swarnajayanti Grameen Swarazgar Yojana (SGSY), Indira Awas Yojana (IAJ), National Social Assistance Programme (NSAP),

Restructured Rural Sanitation Programme, Accelerated Rural Water Supply Programme (ARWSP), have specific funds earmarked for lending solely to women.

Is Micro Finance the Panacea for Poverty Alleviation?

Poverty is a multifaceted phenomenon and can be characterized in terms of the lack of one of more of the following:

(i) Entitlement to food and other basic necessities.

(ii) Access to public provision of economic, social, and human infrastructures.

(iii) Credit, opportunities for income generation, and consumption stabilization.

(iv) Empowerment in both private and public resource allocations.

(v) Access to a social safety net and other resources that help household withstand natural and other shocks, thus safeguarding the very existence of life and families (Khandker, 2001).

Therefore, the extent of poverty alleviation is not defined by the access to credit or other financial services, rather, how is the receiver able to utilize those services to generate sources of revenue.

The most widespread micro financing instrument is micro credit or micro lending, which is the issuance of small, unsecured loans to individuals or groups for the purpose of starting or expanding businesses. Micro financing aims to alleviate poverty by stimulating economic growth through entrepreneurial initiative (Khavul, 2010). But for this effort to be successful, it should be known to the people to whom it is offered, that how to utilize it. It is affected both by the skill level of the entrepreneur and the economic development in the local environment (Khandker, 2001).

Also, as per the UN Bluebook, for financial inclusion, financial services combined with financial literacy and other skill building techniques is imperative.

Gaps

A major underlying assumption in believing micro finance can bring about poverty alleviation is that the low income group has the necessary skill and know-how of setting up a successful business venture (Khavul, 2010).

However, this assumption itself is not very sound. Low income generation group seek out earning opportunities at different avenues, so as not to become specialized. There are two main reasons for it. First, spreading of risk, so that going away of one of the options does not impair their earning capability much and they have other earning avenues open for them. Second, many a times they even do not have the funds to run a task that would fully employ them (Banerjee and Duflo, 2006). This leads to their lack of specialization in a particular type of trade or mode of running business, which in turn creates greater business risk for the borrower.

Also, in the absence of adequate local economic development, in spite of skills, it might be difficult to generate sustained higher incomes.

Thus, many times, the borrowers tend to get worse after getting the credit than better. This is because, the interest rates are high and it becomes difficult to pay back in the absence of a commensurate increase of income. This forms a vicious cycle of poverty.

Penetration of MFIs in India is still lacking. As per the Rural Financial Access Survey (RFAS), even till 2003 79% of the rural population did not have access to formal sources of credit (Basu Priya, 2005). Penetration of MFIs is still not Pan India. Northern states like Nagaland, Mizoram and Arunachal Pradesh are still devoid of much micro finance activity. In many states, penetration is partial (State of the Sector Report, 2009).

The cost of targeting low income population is very high and this affects the financial sustainability of the MFIs. More than a third of the MFIs are making losses. Also, the profit making MFIs majorly are the ones which are large (State of Sector Report, 2009). Due to the increasing pressure on the bottom lines of these institutions, the growth and the penetration these MFIs are reporting seem to be questionable. The question here is whether the deserving people are being targeted or not and whether the objective of financial inclusion actually being met.

Lack of adequate regulation for the micro finance institutions also remains an important area of concern. Many small newly set up institutions, in order to set up themselves, may resort to predatory pricing, which negatively affects the entire MF sector present in that area. The reverse might also be the case. In case of areas which are not tapped, newly set up MFI might charge exorbitantly high interest rates. There are even such cases where the moneylenders just call themselves to be a part of MFI and lend at extremely high interest rates. Such ill practices instead of promoting financial inclusion end up marring the whole effort. The lack of adequate regulation also affects the information disclosure. There is no standardized information disclosure norms followed by the MFIs. Most of the information shared is on a voluntary basis. It not only results in information asymmetry, it also leaves a potential scope for malpractices.

Micro Finance in Other Countries

Micro finance movement gained popularity only after the tremendous success that it met with in Bangladesh. It is a densely populated country having a population of 140 million people out of which about 84% reside in rural areas. Due to changing macroeconomic environment, men and women found them forced into labour markets. This was more pronounced for the female population. The main objective of the micro credit programmes of Bangladesh was to provide these women with a better source of income, (through occupations like poultry, petty trading, weaving, stitching, etc.) and make their lives self-sustainable, economically.

The Grameen Bank model, invented by Mohammad Yunus of Bangladesh in 1976 is one of the most successful MF model in the world. Impetus for this innovative model, for which Mohd. Yunus even won the Nobel Prize for Peace in the year 2006, came from the famine in Bangladesh in 1974. Apart from lending to the poor without collateral for their enterprise, Grameen organization also engages the borrowers in proper membership programme. New members are placed in groups of five, with five to eight groups forming a centre. All members in the centre meet with a loan officer weekly. For the first few weeks, they learn Grameen rules, save $0.02 a week, learn to sign their names, and 5 memorize a set of vows to self-improvement. Each group elects a chair, and each centre elects a chief. New members also must buy a share of stock in Grameen Bank for $2 (Schreiner, 2003). Here, the services were not restricted to financial services of lending, but other important features like habit of saving, education and ethics were also tried to inculcate. This ensured that some contribution is made towards their well-being and upliftment as well. Micro finance activities have enabled the rural females, who were earlier sitting idle at their home, to participate in the economic activities. Income generation by women also led to their empowerment and increased decision-making ability (Afrin Sharmina *et al.*, 2010).

In contrast to the situation in Bangladesh, Thailand is placed in a much better position, in terms of economic development. Thailand's growth is led by banks, where financial services are obtained from commercial banks. This situation is very similar to that in India. The impetus for the micro finance programme came from the crisis in 1997, that led to the government formulating a 'National Micro Finance Master Plan' in the year 2000. The MF sector there is government-driven and is provided by government agencies like Specialized Financial Institutions (SFI). Bank of Agriculture and Agricultural Cooperatives (BAAP), Government Savings Bank (GSB). All these entities form the formal category of MFIs, which are regulated. These account for about 89% of the total credit provided in 2007. Apart from these, there are semi-formal MFIs, like registered cooperatives and Village and Urban Revolving Funds (VRF), and informal institutions like self-help groups. SHGs account only for around 1% of the total credit. (Micro Finance Industry Report Thailand, 2010).

Even in developed countries like USA, UK and Canada, provision of micro finance is present. In USA, the financial exclusion figures were very less (9% in 2006) as compared to the developing countries, and the banks itself sufficed in terms of covering. A civil rights legislation known as the Community Reinvestment Act was established that required banks provide financial inclusion. Whereas in France, a bank account was made a person's legal right. A person refused a bank account could apply to the Bank of France and hold an account (Shetty, V.P., 2006).

The MFI Opportunity and Challenges in India

The Micro Finance Institutions try to bridge the income inequalities by trying to provide financial services to the people belonging to the low income group who are denied access to credit, insurance and other financial services by the commercial financial institutions. The micro finance sector has emerged from the efforts of Non-governmental Organizations (NGOs), and as a response to the failure of existing structures to deliver financial services to the poor.

These models have come up with many innovative and flexible ways of providing financial services to the rural poor who have fluctuating incomes. They have come up with solutions like progressive lending, joint liability and repeated lending, to reduce the risk associated with default. MFI industry is on a high growth trajectory. Sa-Dhan report states that despite the liquidity constraints faced by some MFIs, the client outreach and the loan portfolio has been encouraging. Sa-Dhan also reports that these MFIs have penetrated the 234 (out of 331) poorest of the districts identified by the government. MFIs have also been instrumental in women empowerment as women formed around 93% of their clientele.

Although the results might be encouraging, gaps exist. They are as follows:

(1) Increased concentration of MFI has intensified competition among them, making their financial sustainability difficult. It has resulted in increased loan size, which apart from increasing the risk undertaken, also implies that the extremely poor people are not being targeted.

(2) The loan amount, which is taken as the prime indicator of the success of MFIs, does not guarantee the generation of a poverty alleviating income, they only provide access to credit. There are no indicators for measuring the impact

of micro finance services on the extent of poverty alleviation caused. The data estimated is only about the loan amount and the repayment. However, it might be that the borrower is taking up multiple loans to repay the original one.

(3) Penetration of MFIs is still not Pan India. Northern states like Nagaland, Mizoram and Arunachal Pradesh are still devoid of much micro finance activity. In many states, penetration is partial.

(4) There is a lack of standardization in operations and lack of regulations. This also leads to lack of transparency and lesser availability of data regarding their operations. The data that is available for various reporting and study purposes is more on a voluntary disclosure basis.

Way Forward: Government's Pivotal Role

A way ahead for such endeavors could be to have a more streamlined approach instead of spurring competition among various disaggregated bodies for provision of micro finance services. However, for this to be done, the initiative from the government has to move away from mere regulatory interventions to active shaping up of the micro finance sector in India. Focus on financial inclusion through micro finance activities can be bifurcated into the following:

(1) Access to basic banking — accounts opening and savings.

(2) Access to credit to the low income groups.

(3) Access to micro insurance.

Different regions of the country would be on different levels of maturity in terms of their micro financing needs. The need for micro finance in different regions will be dependent on a number of factors like the income level of the residents, the employment opportunity available, gap between their current earnings and required earnings, entrepreneurial orientation, the kind of financial services already present in the region, and its depth, etc. The parameters mentioned will be different for the different regions and thus the provision of services should also be in line with the needs and suitability. The above parameters broadly will decide that which level of MF services should be focused upon for a particular region.

Also, mere provision of financial services is not sufficient, these have to be coupled with other supporting activities which help in the spurring of economic development. For example, only provision of credit without making of any proper entrepreneurial activity which can generate sustained revenues. Availability of income generation avenues leads to progressively higher level of incomes for the low income group and their absence will only spur increased borrowing without any corresponding increase in the income and can lead to multiple borrowings to repay the same loan (in case multiple MFIs are present in the region), without actually causing any economic development or poverty alleviation.

Similarly, by asking the people to save money will be of no use in their upliftment or well being, if there aren't avenues where they can spend it for constructive use, for example, schools, hospitals, knowledge of basic hygiene, etc. In other words, basic facilities life proper schools, hospitals, and training for skills that increase employability, spreading awareness about hygiene and disease prevention etc. are equally important as the financial services if economic development is being targeted.

The above-mentioned considerations imply that Micro Finance Institutions alone cannot achieve financial inclusion — they act only as facilitators; if large-scale financial inclusion is to be achieved, micro finance services need to be combined with the efforts of Government. The governments' role becomes instrumental here as the necessary impetus for economic activity has to come from the government. Having stated that, it is also clear that a mere central level intervention will not be effective, as the state level and the local level governments will be better positioned to gauge the level of economic activities and future opportunities based upon the skill level of the people. For villages it might also mean taking feedback from the Village Panchayat too.

In fact, here the governing bodies present at the root level should be more instrumental in bringing about the poverty alleviation in their region of governance. They should be made responsible for all the operational activity, and also largely for the success of the programme. In fact, the state/district governments can spur competition among the various regions for better implementation.

A critical issue in front of the government and other MF providers is increasing the penetration, reaching out to the poorest areas while making it financially viable. One of the approaches here could be reaching out through Post Offices. The post offices, which enjoy a nationwide presence, can be leveraged. In fact, this model has already been implemented in UK, where a Post Office Card Account (POCA) is provided to those who are unable to access a bank account (Leeladhar V., 2005).

In fact, a pilot study has already been done in Tamil Nadu and Meghalaya by NABARD on leveraging post offices for simple borrowing and lending operations for the poor. This would have the following impacts:

(1) Bring centralization in the process — authentic data availability and transparency of operations.

(2) Reduce multiple lending from various MFI present in the same region. It will make it easier to study the impact of economic development due to availability of finance.

(3) Improve operational effectiveness. Instead of setting up banks which will have high overheads and pressure on financial viability because of competition among various MFIs.

(4) More importantly, in the pilot done by NABARD, post offices receive the Revolving Fund Assistance from NABARD at 6% and they utilize this fund in lending to the SHG at 9%. This greatly brings down the interest cost, and increases the viability even for the poor.

Measurement of impact of the provision of Micro finance services still remains an area which is to be worked upon. Merely measuring the number of families covered and the size of loans are not adequate. Attempts have to be made to measure the impact of such services on the lives of the people. This would be the true indicator of the extent of financial inclusion achieved, as it is not only the fund access that determines financial inclusion or exclusion, but also the utilization of it.

The long term target of the government should be to spur economic development among the low income groups, uplift them and bring them under the radar of the normal commercial banking system. This would actually result in true financial inclusion. This would also mean that a gradual phasing out of the micro finance services in future would be inevitable. In other words, the micro finance industry should witness an inverted U-shaped growth curve. However, this phasing out may not happen uniformly all over the country, rather it should be a gradual step by step process depending upon the extent of poverty alleviation attained in the specifi regions. So even in this respect, active involvement of government not only at the central level but also at the state and the local levels becomes imperative, so as t provide a continuous monitoring and feedback mechanism on the impact.

References

1. Afrin Sharmina *et al.* (2010), Micro Credit and Rural Women Entrepreneurship Development in Bangladesh: A Multivariate Model, *Journal of Business and Management*, Vol. 16, No. 1, 2010.
2. Banerjee A.B. and Duflo, E. (2006), "The Economic Lives of the Poor," *Journal of Economic Perspectives.*

3. Basu, Priya (2005), "A Financial System for India's Poor", *Economic and Political Weekly.*

4. Beegle, Dehejia, Gatti (2003), *Child Labour, Crop Shocks and Credit Constraints.*

5. Desta, Rafael (2009), Micro Credit for Poverty Alleviation and Fostering Environmentally Sustainable Development: A Review of African Case Studies, *International Journal of Business Research.*

6. Doocy, S. *et al.* (2005), "Outcomes of an Ethiopian Micro Finance Programme and Management Actions to Improve Services", *Journal of Micro Finance.*

7. International Monetary Fund (2005), Micro Finance: A View from the Fund.

8. Leeladhar V. (2005), Speech at Fedbank Hormis Memorial Foundation at Ernakulam.

9. Kazianga Harounan (2005), Income Risk and Schooling Decisions in Burkina Faso.

10. Khabdker Shahid (2001), "Does Micro Finance Really Benefits the Poor?", *Journal Asian Development Bank.*

11. Khavul Susanna (2010), "Micro Finance: Creating Opportunities for the Poor?", *Academy of Management Perspectives.*

12. *Micro Finance Industry Report - Thailand, 2010.*

13. NABARD, Chapter 8, *Micro Finance Institutions.*

14. Sa-Dhan Report, 2009.

15. Schreiner Mark (2003), A Cost-effective Analysis of Grameen Bank of Bangladesh, *Development Policy Review*, 2003, Vol. 21, No. 3.

16. Shetty V.P. (2006) Speech, CMD, IDBI at IDRBT, Hyderabad.

■■■

5 Micro Finance in India — An Imbalanced Growth

Dr. C.L. Dadhich,*
Secretary, Indian Society of Agricultural Eco.

Micro Finance is provision of thrift, credit and other financial services and products of very small amount to the poor in rural, semi-urban and urban areas for enabling them to raise their income levels and improve their standard of living (RBI 2000). Efforts were made in early 1990s to purvey micro finance services through self-help groups (SHGs). In order to augment resources of SHGs, NABARD launched in 1992 a pilot project on self-help group-bank linkage programme (SBLP). This is by far the most popular model of micro finance in India. Later on, micro finance institutions with diverse institutional and legal forms also came on the scene in a big way. The main objective of this paper is to review trend and progress and growth pattern of micro finance movement in India. The paper also suggests measure to smoothen the growth. The analysis is based on the annual information published by NABARD for the year 2008-09 on Micro Finance in India. Though MFI segment accounted for about one-fourth in micro finance sector, very little information is available in this publication. Apparently, majority of MFIs are working as closed shop under the iron curtain and only source of some information is their annual report.

A Remarkable Quantitative Jump

With a humble beginning in 1992 as a pilot project, micro finance movement has made a remarkable progress in terms of number of SHG, number of members and amount financed. Under SBLP alone, as on March 31, 2009, 4.2 million SHGs had outstanding (cumulative) bank loans of Rs. 226.8 billion, with average loan

* Author is Former Director of Rural Economics, Reserve Bank of India, Mumbai.

outstanding per SHG was Rs. 53689 (Table 5.1). As on the reference date about 6.1 million SHGs had savings bank accounts with total savings of Rs. 55.5 billion. During 2008-09, the average savings per SHG with bank works out to Rs. 9,096 (Table 5.2). Thus, the number of SHGs with bank savings were more than SHGs borrowing from banking system. This suggest higher savings potential of poor in rural areas. In all, as on March 31, 2009, more than 80 million poor families were associated with banking agencies under SBLP making it the largest micro finance programme in the world (Government of India, 2010).

Table 5.1: Bank Loans Outstanding Under SBLP (As at End-March)

(Amount in Rs. billion)

Agency (1)	No. of SHGs (in '000)		Outstanding Loans	
	2007-08 (2)	2008-09 (3)	2007-08 (4)	2008-09 (5)
Commercial Banks	2,378	2,831	114.8	161.5
Regional Rural Banks	876	978	44.2	52.2
Co-operative Banks	371	416	11.0	13.1
Total	3,626	4,224	170.0	226.8

Source: NABARD.

Table 5.2: Savings of SHGs with Banks (As at End-March)

(Amount in Rs. billion)

Agency (1)	No. of SHGs (in '000)		Savings of SHGs	
	2007-08 (2)	2008-09 (3)	2007-08 (4)	2008-09 (5)
Commercial Banks	2,811	3,549	20.8	27.7
Regional Rural Banks	1,387	1,629	11.8	19.9
Co-operative Banks	812	943	5.4	7.8
Total	5,010	6,121	38.0	55.5

Source: NABARD.

Pursuant of guidelines issued by RBI in February 2000, stipulating that micro credit extended by bank to individual borrower directly or through any conduct/ intermediary would henceforth be recognised as priority sector lending with freedom to charge any rate of interest, banks extended loans to MFIs for onlending to the poor. Social investors such as SIDBI, NABARD and multilateral banking agencies like IFC and GTZ also extended financial support to MFI sector. These developments gave a big push to MFI sector.

As a result, micro finance delivery through Micro Finance Institutions (MFIs) has emerged as a strong bridge between the banking sector and the rural poor. Though information about SHGs or member financed by MFIs is readily not available, yet funds extended by banking sector to MFIs could be an appropriate measure of their role in micro finance movement. As on March 31, 2009, bank loan outstanding aggregated to Rs. 50 billion against 1,915 MFIs (Table 5.3). Considering the short span of less than two decades of its existence, the progress of micro finance is praiseworthy.

Table 5.3: Bank Loans of MFIs (As at End-March)

(Amount in Rs. billion)

Category of Bank (1)	Loans Disbursed by Banks to MFIs		Outstanding Bank Loans against MFIs	
	2007-08 (2)	2008-09 (3)	2007-08 (4)	2008-09 (5)
Commercial Banks	19.7 (497)	37.2 (522)	27.5 (1,072)	49.8 (1,762)
Regional Rural Banks	0.02 (8)	0.13 (59)	0.04 (24)	0.3 (153)
Co-operative Banks	0.0004 (13)	- (0)	0.0002 (13)	- (0)
Total	19.7 (518)	37.3 (581)	27.5 (1,109)	50.1 (1,915)

-: nil/negligible.

Note: 1. Figures in parentheses represent the number of MFIS.

2. The actual number of FIs would be less as some FIs have availed loans from more than one bank.

Source: NABARD.

Higher Drop-out Rate — A Syndrome of Discontent

While quantitative performance of micro finance sector is quite impressive, it appears qualitative progress is on wane. Drop-out rate or exit rate is a proxy of discontent. Viewed from this measure (Sinha, 2007) in recent period drop-out rate in MFI segment has increased to 11 per cent from 6 per cent during 2002-03. So far micro finance sector is growing faster than 11 per cent, it is easy to mask this alarming exit or drop-out rate but once growth is stabilised and drop-out rate is not arrested by improving qualitative aspects micro finance movement may soon show cracks in quantitative terms as well.

Fair Treatment to Women at a Price

The best part of the micro finance sector is prominence of women in formation and financing of SHGs. The information presented in Table 5.4 reveals that as at end March 2009, 77.6 per cent of SHGs financed have exclusively women members. They accounted for 81.9 per cent of total loans outstanding. The overwhelmingly higher proportion of women in the sector has led to empowerment of women in decision making. This may bring about the social transformation in the long run. However, financial services are gender neutral and excessive dependence on women have adversely impacted the speed of the growth of the movement. This may cause lopsided development of micro finance sector.

Table 5.4: Position of Women SHGs

(Rs. in billion)

	Total SHGs		Exclusive Women SHGs		% age of women SHGs to total SHGs		
Particulars (1)	Year (2)	No. (3)	Amount (4)	No. (5)	Amount (6)	No. (7)	Amount (8)
Saving linked SHGs	2007-08	5009794	37.8	3986093	31.1	79.57	82.12
	2008-09	6121147	55.5	4863921	44.3	79.46	79.96
Loans disbursed	2007-08	1227770	88.5	1040996	74.7	84.79	84.46
	2008-09	1609586	122.5	1374579	105.3	85.39	85.91
Loans Outstanding	31.03.2008	3625941	170.0	2917259	133.4	80.46	78.45
	31.03.2009	4224338	226.8	3277355	185.8	77.58	81.93

Regional Disparities — A Cause of Concern

The number of SHG financed was highest in the southern region (54.0 per cent) distantly followed by eastern region (22.1 per cent), western region (9.8 per cent) and central region (7.9 per cent). Speaking in terms of bank loan outstanding, again southern region topped the list (65.8 per cent) distantly followed by eastern region (13.3 per cent), central region (9.0 per cent) and western region (6.8 per cent). However, juxtaposing with number of poor, the share of bank loan outstanding under micro finance sector was higher only in the southern region while remaining regions have higher share of the poor (Table 5.5).

Table 5.5: Region-wise Number SHG Financed Loan Outstanding and No. of Persons Below Poverty Line 2008-09

Regions (1)	No. of SHGs (2)	% (3)	Bank loan (4)	% (5)	No. of Persons BPL (million) (6)	% (7)
Northern Region	166511	(3.94)	67891.97	(2.99)	223.76	(7.42)
North-eastern Region	117812	(2.79)	46930.53	(2.07)	78.96	(2.62)
Eastern Region	933489	(22.10)	302300.32	(13.33)	873.31	(28.94)
Central Region	332116	(7.86)	204533.13	(9.02)	966.63	(32.02)
Western Region	393499	(9.32)	155114.74	(6.84)	410.08	(13.59)
Southern Region	2280911	(54.00)	1491213.56	(65.75)	462.58	(15.33)
Total	4224338	(100.0)	2267984.25	(100.0)	3017.2	(100.0)

%: Percentage of total.

Source: Micro Finance in India 2008-09 NABARD, BPL: Below Poverty Line.

At the state level, Andhra Pradesh has highest number of SHG financed (28.9 per cent) distantly followed by Tamil Nadu (13.6 per cent), West Bengal (11.2 per cent), Maharashtra (8.4 per cent), Orissa (8.0 per cent) and Karnataka (7.3 per cent). These five states together accounted for 97.4 per cent of the SHGs financed (Table 5.6).

Table 5.6: State-wise Number SHG Financed Loan Outstanding and No. of Persons Below Poverty Line 2008-09

Regions (Rs. million) (1)	No. of SHGs (2)	% (3)	Bank loan BPL (million) (4)	% (5)	No. of Persons (6)	% (7)
Andhra Pradesh	1219311	28.86	890216.81	39.25	126.1	4.18
Arunachal Pradesh	4872	0.122	302.56	0.10	2.03	0.07
Assam	88878	2.10	3285.42	1.45	55.77	(1.85)
Bihar	83444	1.98	45483	2.01	369.15	12.23
Chattisgarh	65827	1.56	31158.01	1.37	90.96	3.01
Delhi	1597	0.04	1248.53	0.06	22.93	0.76
Goa	2828	0.07	1923.01	0.08	2.01	0.06
Gujarat	37105	0.88	10938.49	0.48	90.69	3.00

Haryana	15312	0.36	12414.37	0.55	32.1	1.06
Himachal Pradesh	32752	0.78	9633.33	0.42	6.36	0.21
Jammu & Kashmir	912	0.02	456.58	0.02	5.85	0.19
Jharkhand	40824	0.97	19033.39	0.84	116.39	3.86
Karnataka	309097	7.32	161361.56	7.11	138.89	4.60
Kerala	176153	4.17	95093.05	4.19	49.6	1.64
Madhya Pradesh	34938	0.83	13254.94	0.58	249.68	8.26
Maharashtra	353566	8.37	142253.23	6.27	317.38	10.52
Manipur	3410	0.08	708.17	0.03	3.95	0.13
Meghalaya	3115	0.07	1139.32	0.05	4.52	0.15
Mizoram	2278	0.05	1392.72	0.06	1.18	0.04
Nagaland	883	0.02	891.12	0.04	3.99	0.13
Orissa	335811	7.95	132428.42	5.84	178.49	5.92
Punjab	17981	0.43	7484.53	0.33	21.63	0.72
Rajasthan	97957	2.32	36654.63	1.62	134.89	(4.47
Sikkim	3975	0.09	3935.60	0.17	1.14	0.04
Tamil Nadu	576350	13.64*	344542.14	15.19*	145.62	4.83
Tripura	10401	0.25	3705.62	0.16	6.38	0.21
Uttar Pradesh	112620	2.67	65033.92	2.87	590.03	19.56
Uttarakhand	118731	2.81	95086.26	4.19	35.96	1.19
West Bengal	472556	11.19	105043.98	4.63	208.36	6.19
Andaman and Nicobar Islands	854	0.02	311.53	0.01	0.92	0.03
Chandigarh	-		-		0.74	0.02
Dadra and Nager Haveli	-		-		0.84	0.03
Diu	-		-		0.21	0.006
Lakshadweep	-		-		0.11	0.003
Pondicherry	-		-		2.37	0.08
India	4224338	100.0	2267984.25	100.0	3017.2	100.0

%: Percentage to total

Source: Micro Finance in India 2008-09, NABARD.

So far bank loan outstanding is concerned again, Andhra Pradesh topped the list with 39.3 per cent distantly followed by Tamil Nadu (15.2 per cent), Karnataka (7.1 per cent), Maharashtra (6.3 per cent) and West Bengal (4.6 per cent). Juxtaposing state-wise number of poor only Andhra Pradesh, Tamil Nadu and Kerala have higher share of loan outstanding as compared to share of poor. Strikingly enough, lower share of loan outstanding was noticed in the states of Bihar, Madhya Pradesh, Uttar Pradesh, Maharashtra, Rajasthan and West Bengal. This suggests that micro finance sectors presence has not followed the incidence of the poverty in the country. While micro finance sector is more in the presence in the affluent states poverty ridden states have not got their due still. Thus, imbalanced growth of micro finance sector suggests that it has not dedicated itself to the poor in the country.

Lion's Share of Commercial Banks

Of the total outstanding loans aggregating to Rs. 276.8 billion (both SBLP + MFI) commercial banks top the list with Rs. 211.3 billion constituting 76.3 per cent of the total bank outstanding distantly followed by RRBs Rs. 52.5 billion (19.0 per cent) and co-operative banks Rs. 13.0 billion (4.7 per cent). Similarly, in terms of SHGs financed, commercial banks ranked first with 2.8 million (66.6 per cent) distantly followed by RRBs 1.0 million (23.8 per cent) and co-operative banks 0.4 million (9.6 per cent). The average loan outstanding per SHG at Rs.57,037 was the highest in case of commercial banks to a low of Rs. 31,460 per SHG in the case of the co-operative banks. Surprisingly enough, RRBs and co-operative banks which are supposed to take care of the poor have the secondary position in regard to micro finance. Apparently, micro finance is on the back burner of these pro-poor banks.

Inadequate Funding

It may be observed from Table 5.7 that during 2008-09 loans amounting to Rs. 122.5 billions were disbursed to 1.6 million SHGs under SBLP. The average loan per SHG worked out to Rs. 76,562. Presuming 20 members per SHG, average loan per member is around Rs. 3,828. Keeping in view, requirement of one dollar income per day per person, a family of 5 members may have annual income of US $1,825, i.e., Rs. 79,025. The average loan amount of Rs. 3,828 is too inadequate to help him to cross the poverty line. Thus, average loan amount is far inadequate to purchase an asset generating reasonable income to meet basic necessities let alone the higher standard of living. At the disaggregate level, average loans disbursed by RRBs and cooperative banks was far below the average level thus making any worthwhile investment.

Table 5.7: Agency-wise SHG-Bank Linkage Programme (As at End-March)

(Amount in Rs. billion)

Agency (1)	No. of SHGs (in '000) 2007-08 (2)	No. of SHGs (in '000) 2008-09 (3)	Bank Loan Disbursed 2007-08 (4)	Bank Loan Disbursed 2008-09 (5)
Commercial Banks	735	1,005	5,404	8,061
Regional Rural Banks	328	406	2,652	3,193
Co-operative Banks	165	199	794	999
Total	1,228	1,610	8,849	12,254

Source: NABARD.

Limited Micro Finance Services

Under the SBLP, there were only two products, viz., loans and thrift. Other financial services required by the poor such as, Insurance remittance, etc. were only on papers. Few MFIs have, of course, started these services (Nagarajan, 2010) but it may take long time for other MFIs to meet the requirements of poor to the satisfactory level. So far savings are concerned, only one saving product has been provided by almost all the banks under the linkage programme. While poor requires a variety of savings products to meet their different types of requirement like marriage of daughter, housing, old age pension, etc. (Dadhich, 2000). Similarly, insurance products are also stereotyped without taking into consideration the needs and requirement of the poor. In the absence of proper risk hedging mechanism like life and health insurance, livestock and asset insurance policies the poor stand to lose heavily, which ultimately traps them into a deeper and vicious cycle of poverty (Gunarajan, 2007). Furthermore, loan products do not have subtle diversification, either it is first loan or a repeat loan. The purpose-wise loan products are rare in place. Not only that savings and loan products are stereotyped. Alarming gap between the rate of interest paid on savings and change on loans makes savings an unattractive proposition. As a result, despite wide presence of micro finance sector in the country, rural savings still continue to remain in unorganized sector with accompanying risks if not remained untapped.

Socio-economic Impact of Micro Finance

A recent study conducted by National Council by Applied Economic Research in six major states revealed that implementation of SBLP has by and large improved the access to credit by the rural poor. Empowerment of women was also noticed (NCAER, 2008). However, an evaluation study by Reserve Bank of India on implementation of SBLP pointed out that there was enough scope for improvement in maintenance of accounts. It also brought out that rotation of group leaders was generally not followed (Government of India, 2010). Needless to add that non-rotation of group leaders and poor maintenance of accounts may sooner or later strengthen vested interests and result into exploitation of other members if not the embezzlement of funds. The situation in MFI approach is also far from satisfactory. MFIs have been under attack from various quarters. Their loan recovery practices have been questioned and their interest rates described as exorbitant (Sinha, 2007). A majority of MFIs started their journey with social motives but eventually turned into commercial entities (Ghosh, 2010). Of late, commercial investors such as private equity funds, etc. have influenced operations of MFIs. The quest of some of the MFIs to raise resources through capital market may further drift their mission to a significant extent if they are not able to strike balance between their social and commercial goals. It is worthwhile to note that micro finance programme was envisaged to achieve economic development of the poor through social development. In this context, cardinal principles of Micro Finance need to be given overriding priority (Yunus, 1982). Very little has been done towards family planning, fruit and vegetable growing, tree production, literacy, construction of biogas community plants and pit latrine to keep pollution-free environment.

Growing Default Menace

Because of the intrinsic strength of SHG and peer pressure, default in micro finance was unheard of, for long. However, it may be observed from the data presented in Table 5.8 that percentage of non-performing assets to outstanding loan was about 2.9 per cent at the aggregate level. It was as high as 6.8 per cent in case of co-operative banks followed by RRBs (4.2 per cent) and public sector banks (2.4 per cent). However, incidence of NPAs was lowest at 1.7 per cent in case of private sector banks. It is relevant to note that proportion of NPA to outstanding is a crude tool and at times do not give the true picture. The proper measure is NPA to demand (loan due). Nonetheless, in case of about 10 per cent of the reporting banks recovery, percentage was below 50 per cent, 2.21 per cent banks between 50 to 79 per cent and between 80 to 94 per cent only in case of 38.2 per cent banks. The recovery of above 95 per cent was recorded only in 29.6 per cent of reporting banks (Table 5.9). Obviously, micro finance sector is no longer a safe heaven for lending. Perhaps, higher burden of interest on loans is affecting financial position of the borrower and ultimately eroding the effectiveness of social collaterals. The absence of proper insurance cover might have also accentuated the default rate in micro finance sector. At times, SHGs were used by financing banks to recover their sticky loans (Dadhich, 2001).

Table 5.8: Agency-wise NPAs of Bank Loans to SHGs

(Amount in Rs. Million)

Agency	NPAs as on 31 March 2009			
	Total No. of Banks Reported Data on NPAs	Outstanding Loans against SHGs	Amount of NPAs	% of NPAs to Outstanding Bank Loans
(1)	(2)	(3)	(4)	(5)
Commercial Banks (Public Sector)	26	150866.5	3632.7	2.4
Commercial Banks (Private Sector)	12	13769.3	238.3	1.7
Regional Rural Banks (RRBs)	72	42034.6	1777.9	4.2
Co-operative Banks	182	8940.0	609.7	6.8
Total	292	215610.4	6258.6	2.9

Source: NABARD.

Table 5.9: Recovery Performance — Agency-wise (All SHGs)

Agency reported recovery data	No. of Banks	No. of banks based on percentage distribution of recovery performance of bank loans to SHGs as on 31 March 2009			
		=/> 95%	80-94%	50-79%	< 50%
(1)	(2)	(3)	(4)	(5)	(6)
Commercial Banks (Public Sector)	25	6	12	7	0
Commercial Banks (Private Sector)	7	5	1	0	1
Regional Rural Banks	65	12	31	15	7
Co-operative Banks	170	56	58	37	19
Total	267	79	102	59	27
Percentage of Banks		29.6	38.2	22.1	10.1

Source: NABARD.

Dismal Share of Poor in Micro Finance Sector

Micro finance programme was initially envisaged to alleviate poverty through the self-help groups. However, the share of micro finance sector in Government-sponsored programme, viz., Swarnjayanti Gram Swarozgar Yojana (SGSY) during 2008-09 was around 25.8 per cent in terms of loan amount outstanding. In terms of number of SHGs, the share was little lower at 23.1 per cent. So far bank loans disbursed is concerned, SHGs involved in SGSY were 16.4 per cent and amount disbursed was 16.5 per cent. The lower share of SGSY in disbursements as compared to outstanding indicates about slowing down of the poverty alleviation programme under micro finance sector (Table 5.10). Thus, three-fourths of SHGs were not involved in Government-sponsored programme. About one-fifth of the all poor households are currently receiving micro finance services or at least micro credit. Needless to add that slower progress is being made in reaching out to poor households (Ghate, 2007). The poor performance of micro finance sector in government-sponsored poverty alleviation programme is a matter of serious concern particularly when this sector is expected to reach out to the poorer sections of the society.

Table 5.10: Overall Progress under Micro Finance during the Last Three Years

(Rs. in billion)

Particulars		2006-07		2007-08		2008-09	
		No. of SHGs	Amount	No. of SHGs	Amount	No. of SHGs	Amount
Savings of SHGs with Banks as on 31st March	Total SHGs	4160584	351.27	5009794	378.5	6121147	554.6
	Out of which SGSY	956317	75.75	1203070	80.9	1505581	156.3
	Percentage of SGSY to total	(23.0)	(21.6)	(24.0)	(21.4)	(24.6)	(28.2)
Bank loans disbursed to SHGs during the year	Total SHGs	1105749	657.03	1227770	884.9	1609586	1225.3
Out of which SGSY	188962	141.1	246649	186.7	264653	201.5	
	Percentage of SGSY to total	(17.1)	(21.5)	(20.1)	(21.0)	(16.4)	(16.5)

Bank loans outstanding with SHGs as on March 31	Total SHGs	2894505	1236.6	3625941	1699.9	4224338	2267.9
	Out of which SGSY	687212	327.3	916978	481.6	976887	586.1
	Percentage of SGSY to total	(23.7)	(26.5)	(25.3)	(28.3)	(23.1)	(25.8)

Source: Micro Finance in India 2008-09, NABARD.

The foregoing analysis brings to the fore that about 11 per cent of the members are leaving the programme due to unsatisfactory level of micro finance services. Regional and intra regional disparities in implementation of the programme have also impacted the progress adversely. Excessive dependence on the women has made this a lopsided programme. In the absence of other financial services like micro insurance, remittances, etc., this is merely a micro credit programme rather than a micro finance programme. Little attention was given on the social aspects like family planning, literacy, growing of fruits and vegetables to improve the nutritional in take. As a result, the benefits of credit could remain for long. The higher interest rate on loans has impacted the financial position of borrower leading to default syndrome. At the same time, lower interest rate on saving deposits discouraged not only members to save in organized financial market, but forced MFIs to mobilize resources from out side. The poor financial intermediation will have far-reaching impact on the sustainability of the programme. The lower participation of micro finance sector in poverty alleviation programme may destabilize the vary base of this sector in the long run.

Policy Implications

In order to improve the sustainability of this programme, it is imperative to bestow higher attention on the social development of the borrower. As the saying goes, by giving fish to person, he will eat for one day but by teaching him art of fishing he will eat fish forever. Similarly by giving credit to a poor, he will make comfortable living for few days but developing human resources through literacy, vocational training, nutritional intake etc., will enable him to make his life comfortable forever. Reasonable interest rate on loans and deposits or reasonable intermediation margins will not only reduce the dependence on outside sources like NABARD and capital market, but will improve the financial viability of the borrower and that will go long way to combat rising trends of non-performing assets. As micro financial services are gender neutral, it is high time that male poor are also encouraged to form self-help groups to make it a holistic programme for the entire family rather than lopsided development of the family. Concerted efforts are also needed to reduce regional and intra regional imbalances in the growth of micro finance sector through wholehearted participation in poverty alleviation programme. Last but not least important is to put in place a sound system to collection and compilation of information from MFIs to regulate them effectively. Needless to say that micro finance is last hope of India.

References

1. Dadhich, C.L. (2003), Micro Finance — An Innovation in Banking with the Poor, *CAB Calling*, July-December.
2. Dadhich, C.L. (2002), Relevance of Micro Finance in Socio-economic Resurgence in Mumbai, *The City*, August-Sept.
3. Dadhich, C.L. (2000), Lessons from the Micro Credit Experiences of India, http://www.apraca.th.com./sign-Guestbook/Infomarket/Lessons from 1the Micro Credit/body lessons from the micro credit.html).
4. Dadhich, C.L. (2002), Micro Finance Movement for Poverty Alleviation in India — A Review, *Financing Agriculture*, Volume 34, April-June.
5. Dadhich, C.L. (2001), Banking with the Poor — Need for New Savings Linked Products, *22nd Bank Economist's Conference*, Oriental Bank of Commerce.
6. Dadhich, C.L. (2001), Micro Finance — A Panacea for Poverty Alleviation — A Case Study of Oriental Bank Grameen Project in India, *Indian Journal of Agricultural Economics*, Conference Number July-September.
7. Dadhich, C.L. (2000), Repackaging Micro Credit Programme, *Business Line*, May 2.
8. Dadhich, C.L. (2000), Financing Micro Entrepreneurs: Lessons from Kenya, *Financial Express*, February 08.
9. Dadhich, C.L. (2000), Dossier on Micro Finance, *Credit Information Review* RBI, January.
10. Dadhich, C.L. (1999), Financing Micro Entrepreneurs: Need for Multi-agency Approach, *Asia Pacific Rural Finance*, October-December.
11. Dadhich, C.L. (1995), Bangladesh Grameen Bank (Pros and Cons), *Economic Times*, January 12.
12. NABARD (1999), Task Force on Supportive Policy and Regulatory Framework for Micro Finance.
13. NCAER (2008), Impact and Sustainability of SHG-Bank Linkage Programme
14. NABARD (2009), Micro Finance in India.

15. NABARD (2010), Annual Report.
16. RBI (2000), Report on Micro Credit.
17. RBI (2009), Report on Trend and Progress of Banking in India.
18. Government of India (2010,) Economic Survey.
19. Gunarajan Sai (2007), Micro Insurance, in Prabhu Ghate (2007) *op. cit.*
20. Ghosh Chandra Shekhar (2010), MFIs Need to Introspect, *Economic Times*, April 20.
21. Ghate Prabhu (2007), Micro Finance in India A State of Sector Report Sage Publications India Pvt. Ltd.
22. Handy Danial C., Paul Holden and Vassill Prokepenko (2002), Micro Finance Institutions and Public Policy, IMF Working Paper, 02/159.
23. Sinha, Frances (2007), "Social Performance in India Micro Finance" in Prabhu Ghate 2007, *op. cit.*
24. Sinha Sanjay (2007), "MFI Performance: Efficiency with Growth" in Prabhu Ghate (2007) *op. cit.*
25. Nagarajan, Rema (2010), Ekols Sound, *Times of India*, 24.4.2010.
26. Puhazhendhi, V. and Satyasai, K.J.S. (2000), Micro Finance for Rural Poor, NABARD.
27. Singhal Amit and Duggal Bikram (2002), Extending Banking to the Poor in India, ICICsocial initiatives.org.
28. Scott-BW (1992), Banking with the Poor, The Foundation for Development Corporation, Australia.
29. Yunus Muhammad (1987), Credit for Self-employment: A Fundamental Human Right Grameen Bank, Bangladesh.
30. Yunus Muhammad (1982), Grameen Bank Project in Bangladesh.
31. Yunus Muhammad (1992), Strategy for the Decade of Nineties, Grameen Bank, Bangladesh.
32. Yunus Muhammad (1983), Group-based Savings and Credit for Rural Poor, Grameen Bank, Bangladesh.

6 The Looming Micro Finance Crisis and Its Implications for the Rural Sector

Vijaya Venkatesh*
Director, Research Division, ISAE

Micro Finance — An Overview

Since the 1970s, developing countries including India have increasingly focused on micro finance to facilitate the access of poor households to financial services like credit, savings and insurance. The rural population in India constituting more than 60 per cent of the total population pined for timely and adequate availability of credit. Micro finance has, in recent times, come to be recognized and accepted as one of the new development paradigms for alleviating poverty through social and economic empowerment of the poor, with focus on empowering women. Experiences of different anti-poverty and other welfare programmes within the country and elsewhere have shown that the key to its success lies in the participation of community based organizations at the grassroots level. People's participation in credit delivery, recovery and linking of formal credit institutions to borrowers through the intermediation of Self-help Groups (SHGs) has been recognised as a supplementary mechanism for providing credit support to the rural poor (Puhazhendi and Badatya, 2002). The implementation of Swarnjayanti Gram Swarozgar Yojana

---

Director of Research, Indian Society of Agricultural Economics, Mumbai. Paper presented at the National Seminar on "Rethinking on Rural Finance in the Current Scenario" organised by the Oriental Institute of Management, Mumbai, on September 24-25, 2010.

(SGSY) in April 1999 to mobilize physical and financial resources in the rural areas has also facilitated the improvement of income levels of many rural households. It is a holistic programme of self-employment covering the implementation of micro enterprises through organization of the poor into self-help groups (SHGs), provision of timely and adequate credit, training, technology and marketing. In fact, micro finance has made great strides during the last few years and is emerging as an influential and high potential in its own right. C. Rangarajan's Committee on financial inclusion reported that micro finance institutions (MFIs) could play a significant role in facilitating inclusion, as they are uniquely positioned to reaching out to the rural poor.

Definition of Micro Finance

Micro Credit/Finance is defined as provision of thrift, credit and other financial services and products of very small amount to the poor in rural, semi-urban and urban areas for enabling them to raise their income levels and improve living standards. The loans and credit extended are typically small ("micro"). They are provided in varying contexts, either to individuals or groups, ranging from personal micro credit, to small enterprise support and rural finance. The declaration of the Micro Credit Summit held in Washington D.C. in 1977 defined micro credit programmes as 'those extending small loans to poor people for self-employment projects that generate income, allowing them to care for themselves and their families' (Dhandapani, 2009). The task force on supportive policy and regulatory framework for micro finance defined micro finance as "provision of thrift, credit, and other financial services and products of very small amounts to raise the income levels of clients, and improve their living standards." (NABARD, 1999).

Nowadays, micro finance represents something more than micro credit. Micro finance is a financial service of small quantity provided by financial institutions (FIs) to the poor. The institutions that provide micro finance and credit services are diverse, including non-governmental organisations (NGOs), credit unions, non-bank financial intermediaries, and commercial banks. These financial services may include savings, credit, insurance, leasing money transfer, equity transaction, etc. Thus, micro finance refers to the entire range of financial and non-financial services including skill upgradation and entrepreneurship development, rendered to the poor for enabling them to overcome poverty (Nagayya and Rao, 2009). Micro finance providers in India can be classified under three broad categories: formal, semi-formal, and informal. The formal banking sector constitutes the first category while the semi-formal group consists of a variety of MFIs and SHGs. Informal providers, on the other hand, are not legal entities and include moneylenders and various social networks. Today, semi-formal and informal lenders dominate the sector (Tarique and Thakur, 2007).

There has been a spectacular growth in the number of MFIs and their providing succour to the poor in the last few years. In 1997, there were an estimated 618 MFIs which reached 13.4 million people including 7.6 million of the poorest with current loan whereas 2007 saw 3,552 MFIs reaching 154 million people including 106 million of the poorest (*Economic Times*, April 2, 2009). Thus, the country's micro credit landscape is likely to witness rapid growth with MFIs increasingly expanding their service portfolio by adding insurance products, savings-linked schemes and credit facilities for rural dwellers and small entrepreneurs (*Economic Times*, January 18, 2010).

Micro Finance in Rural Areas

The SHG-Bank Linkage Movement which took off in 1992, is today the largest in the world. It is recognized as an effective tool for extending access to formal financial services to the unbanked rural poor. It is a major plank of the strategy for delivering financial services to the poor in a sustainable manner. Initially, there was a slow progress in the programme upto 1999 as only 32,995 groups were credit linked during the period 1992 to 1999. Since then the programme has been growing rapidly and the number of SHGs financed has increased from 1.98 lakh in 2001-02 to more than 5.53 lakh in 2007-08 and 10.81 lakh in 2008-09 (Table 6.1). With the cumulative increase in the number of credit linked SHGs to 47,07,415, the loan disbursement aggregated Rs. 22,679.84 crore as on 31st March, 2009. The bank loan disbursed to new and existing SHGs aggregated Rs. 5,679.93 crore in 2009 as against Rs. 968.70 crore and Rs. 4633.42 crore during the years 2007 and 2008 respectively.

Table 6.1: Growth Trends in the SHGs Financed During Last Few Years

Year	No. of SHGs financed during the year (lakh)	Cumulative No. of SHGs financed (lakh)
2001-02	1.98	4.61
2002-03	2.56	7.17
2003-04	3.62	10.79
2004-05	5.39	16.18
2005-06	6.20	22.38
2006-07	6.86	29.25
2007-08	5.53	34.77
2008-09	10.81	47.07

Source: NABARD Annual Reports (various years).

Encouraged by the success, the programme has been adopted by State Governments as a major poverty alleviation strategy. It has also led to the emergence of MFIs as a bridge between the banking sector and the rural poor. The overall progress of micro finance programme during the last three years is given in Table 6.2.

Table 6.2: Overall Progress of Micro Finance During 2007-2009

(Rs. in crore)

Particulars	2007		2008		Per cent growth (2007-08)		2009		Per cent growth (2008-09)	
	No.	Amount	No.	Amount	No. of SHGs	Amount	No.	Amount	No.	Amount
(1)	(2)	(3)	(4)	(5)	(6)	(7)	(8)	(9)	(10)	(11)
Self-help Groups										
Bank loans disbursed	1105749 (188962)	6570.39 (1411.02)	1227770 (246649)	8849.26 (1857.74)	11.0 (30.5)	34.7 (31.7)	1609586 (264653)	12253.51 (2015.32)	31.1 (7.3)	38.5 (8.5)
Bank loans outstanding	2894505 (687212)	12366.49 (3273.03)	3625941 (916978)	16999.91 (4816.87)	25.3 (33.4)	37.5 (47.2)	4224338 (976887)	22679.84 (5861.72)	16.5 (6.5)	33.4 (21.7)
Savings of SHGs with banks	4160584 (956317)	3512.71 (757.50)	5009794 (1203070)	3785.39 (809.51)	20.4 (25.8)	7.8 (6.9)	6121147 (1505581)	5545.62 (1563.38)	22.2 (25.1)	46.5 (93.1)
Micro Finance Institutions										
Bank loans disbursed	334	1151.56	518	1970.15	55.1	71.1	581	3732.33	12.2	89.4
Bank loans outstanding	550	1584.48	1109	2748.94	101.6	73.5	1915	5009.09	72.7	82.2
Savings of SHGs with banks	-	-	-	-	-	-	-	-	-	-

Source: Status of Micro Finance in India 2008-09, NABARD.
Figures in parentheses indicate the share of SHG covered under SGSY during the year.

As on March 31, 2009, 61.21 lakh SHGs were having saving bank accounts with the banking sector with outstanding savings of Rs. 5,545.62 crore as against 50.09 lakh SHGs having savings of Rs. 3,785.39 crore as on March 31, 2008 registering a growth rate of 22 per cent and 46.5 per cent in 2009 over the previous year. During 2008-09, bank credit of Rs. 12,253.51 and Rs. 3732.33 crore was disbursed to 16.09 lakh SHGs (including 2.65 lakh under SGSY) and 581 MFIs respectively as against Rs. 8,849.26 crore and Rs. 1,970.15 crore disbursed to 12.28 lakh SHGs (including 2.46 lakh under SGSY) and 518 MFIs in 2007-08, respectively. Thus, the coverage of poor households has increased to more than 8.6 crore in 2008-09 as against 7.01 crore poor households in 2007-08. The SHG-Bank Linkage Programme has greatly transformed the whole range of institutions — Government, banks, NGOs and development institutions, in their approach towards development of poor. The programme is growing steadily and it is targeted to achieve a coverage of 100 lakh SHGs much before 2015 (NABARD, 2009-10). SHG lending to members has, however, been reportedly at interest rates ranging between 15 per cent and 24 per cent. Dr. C. Rangarajan has recently remarked that while MFIs have an important role to play in financial inclusion, the high interest rates which they charge could hamper the cause. Besides commercial banks could also make their rural and semi-urban lending more effective by being more farmer-friendly, ensure simplification of procedures to grant loans to small borrowers and implantation of the business facilitator and correspondent model.

Regional Imbalances

It is clearly evident from Table 6.3 that there has been a concentration of SHGs in southern region in 2004-05. Since 2005-06 with concerted efforts and strategic moves, this trend has been reversed to a certain extent. The year 2006-07 witnessed the spread of micro finance programme in resource poor regions of the country indicating a marked shift from its initial concentration in the southern region. Out of the total SHGs linked during the year 62 per cent were in states other than southern states during 2007-08. The spread of SHGs in hilly regions, particularly in the North-eastern region, is poor. One of the reasons is that the population density in hilly areas is often low and the banking network is weak. There is a need to evolve SHG models suited to the local context of such areas. In March 2001, 71 per cent of the linked SHGs were from Southern Region consisting of Andhra Pradesh, Karnataka, Kerala and Tamil Nadu. The share of Southern region has come down progressively over the years but it is still at 44 per cent. Many states such as Uttar

Table 6.3: Regional Shares in SHGs Linkage

Region	SHGs Linked (March 2004)		SHGs Linked (March 2005)		SHGs Linked (March 2006)		SHGs Linked (March 2007)		SHGs Linked (March 2008)	
	No. of groups	Per cent share	No. of groups	Per cent share	No. of groups	Per cent share	No. of groups	Per cent share	No. of groups	Per cent share
(1)	(2)	(3)	(4)	(5)	(6)	(7)	(8)	(9)	(10)	(11)
Northern	52396	4.9	86028	5.3	133097	6	182018	6	230740	6.6
North Eastern	12278	1.1	34238	2.1	62517	3	91754	3	119857	3.4
Eastern	158237	14.7	265628	16.4	394351	18	525881	18	372289	19.3
Central	127009	11.8	197365	12.2	267915	12	332729	11	405707	11.7
Western	54815	5.1	96266	6.0	166254	7	270447	9	374561	10.8
Southern	674386	62.5	939941	58.1	1214431	54	1522144	52	1674811	48.2
Total	1079091	100	1618456	100	2238565	100	2924973	100	3477965	100

Sources: NABARD Annual Reports, Ghate 2008, Srinivasan, 2009.

Pradesh and Bihar with high incidence of poverty have shown poor performance under the programme. The spread of the SHG-Bank Linkage Programme in different regions has been uneven on account of various factors like proactive role of State Governments, presence of well performing NGOs, socio-cultural factors, better performance of SHGs, etc.

NABARD, in association with GTZ, conducted a study, in 2005, on the comparative performance of SHG-Bank linkage programme *vis-à-vis* other priority sector credit. The findings are based on the data received from 27 commercial banks, 192 RRBs and 114 cooperative banks participating in the programme. One of the important observations of the study was that 1.44 million SHGs had loans outstanding of Rs. 4,200 crore with the banking system, 2.63 million SHGs had saving accounts with the banks and the savings outstanding was Rs. 2,391 crore. To cover all the 50 million odd poor households in India, the existing number of SHGs will have to be more than doubled and the extent of credit to the members of each SHG will have to be increased substantially.

The present model of financial inclusion, however, for the most part is too narrowly focused on certain groups like the Government beneficiaries of Social Security Pension Scheme and the NREGP to become viable and is too policy-driven than market-driven. Thus, financial inclusion needs to be all inclusive and cover every segment of the rural population else it will not be sustainable. The four factors are driving purely commercial banks in places as widespread as India, South Africa, Brazil and Egypt to use the existing branch infrastructure to go down the market to tap lower income retail clientele. They are: (i) competition is driving banks into new markets, (ii) the excellent repayment rates micro finance has demonstrated make it an attractive proposition, (iii) banks are seeking to pump more product through their infrastructure and (iv) finally the advent of new technologies that promise to make smaller transactions more cost-effective. For these reasons, commercial banks are now seeing the poor as a viable and even attractive market.

Emerging Issues

The banking sector in India effectively covers about 10 to 15 per cent of the total population and the large majority, particularly in the rural areas, stand outside of the system. Notwithstanding the persistent Government and RBI policy efforts through cooperation multi-agency approach involving the RRBs, LABS, Bank-SHG Linkages, Branch licensing policy and the Lead Bank Scheme, the effective access to banking in the rural areas, whatever be the reasons has remained highly limited, high cost and inefficient. Mostly, the various segments of population in the rural areas including the middle classes and the rich have not been integrated into the banking system within its intermediation role. Thus, it is said that what is needed, in the Indian context is financial integration and not this type of financial inclusion.

The major issues arising from the developments in the micro finance sector during the last two years are: the potential for mission drift in pursuit of vigorous growth, the high risks that are inherent in fast paced growth of organizations that do not have adequate internal checks and controls, the aspirations of majority of NGO sectors to get transformed into MFIs and the impact that this could have on savings by people in their groups, the heightened interest in urban micro finance and the resultant competition increasing the risks of MFIs and their funders. The other issues are the relative ease with which the funds flow into the sector at the top end and the difficulties faced by the players in the middle rungs. There is a certain level of discomfort among banks in expanding their portfolio of bulk loans to the smaller MFIs on account of their perceptions of governance, transparency, quality of information and reputation risk. Not surprisingly, the Banana Skins Survey Report highlighted managing technology, management quality, corporate governance, staffing and competition as the key risks in Asian micro finance. It expresses strong doubts among micro finance practitioners, investors and observers about the ability of many MFIs to adapt to new demands while still retaining their social objects (Srinivasan, 2009).

Conclusion

The past few years have seen the entire micro finance sector grow exponentially and the Indian micro finance industry is characterized by a multiplicity of micro finance providers dispersed across the country. These players belong to diverse institutional forms — NBFIs-MFIs, co-operative societies, not-for-profit companies (under Section 25 of the Companies Act, 1956), trusts — all adhering to different laws and regulations. Complexity is bedeviling the Indian government's attempt to regulate the micro finance sector. In recent months, there has been a flurry of reports about some micro finance institutions (MFIs) offering loans to women without ascertaining their ability to repay, about their staff coercing repayments, about women taking multiple loans to keep up with onerous weekly repayment schedules, etc. Studies have asserted "the quest for rapid growth could lead a company or industry to not realize the bubble they have been building up during this growth phase. While there is no concrete evidence of a bubble as yet, a bubble in the near future cannot be completely ruled out. Thus if MFIs in India can ensure sustained growth through a strong self-regulated mechanism to ensure that a bubble does not come in the way of servicing the millions of customers who need micro credit, we believe that credit can definitely be given to the MFIs for learning from others' mistakes" (Roza, 2010). An analysis of members' loan exposure levels versus their repayment capability needs to be conducted. Development of micro finance sector is one of the important means for facilitating inclusive growth.

Our efforts should be, therefore, to encourage the micro finance sector to grow and reach out to as many people as possible, keeping in mind the need to ensure that the rates of interest are reasonable and recovery practices fair and transparent. The financial inclusion initiatives should focus on coverage of more remote areas and the excluded people. The financial inclusion funds could be accessed by the banks and MFIs to part fund their initial investment costs for expansion to remote areas. Where technology options are available for remote area banking, the costs of initial investment could be met out the Financial Inclusion Technology Fund (Srinivasan, 2009). These measures will enable the micro finance to responsibly serve the micro finance needs of the Indian market without causing a bubble.

References

1. Micro Finance, *Banana Skins*, 2008, http://www.cgap.org
2. "Micro Finance Institutions Needs Succour", *The Economic Times*, July 2, 2009.
3. "Micro Credit to Double as Rural Banks", *The Economic Times*, January 18, 2010.
4. Dhandapani, C. (2009), Micro Finance: SHG-Bank Linkage Programme, SEDME, Vol. 36, No. 4, December.
5. Ghate, Prabhu *et al.* (2008), Micro Finance India — State of the Sector Report 2007, Sage Publications India Pvt. Ltd., New Delhi.
6. National Bank for Agriculture and Rural Development (NABARD), Status of Micro Finance in India — 2008-09, Mumbai.
7. Nagayya, D. and D. Koteswara Rao, "Micro Finance and Support Organisations in the Southern States", SEDME, Vol. 36, No. 4, December 2009.

8. Puhazhendi, V. and K.C. Badatya (2002), SHG-Bank Linkage Programme for Rural Poor — An Impact Assessment, National Bank for Agriculture and Rural Development, Mumbai.

9. Roza, Daniel (2010), "Is There a Micro Finance Bubble in South India?", *Micro Finance Focus*, January 10.

10. Srinivasan, N. (2009), Micro Finance India — State of the Sector Report 2008, Sage Publications India Pvt. Ltd., New Delhi.

11. Tarique, M.D. and Ranjan Kumar Thakur (2007), Growth of Micro Finance Credit in India — An Evaluation, 90th Conference of the Indian Economic Association, New Delhi.

12. Trends in Micro Finance 2010-15, Microned/Triodos Facet www.micro-ned.nl; www.triodosfacet.nl

■■■

7

Micro Finance: Practice and Lessons for the Future

Mr. Shri Shariar Karim
Corporate Trainer

AN "OVERVIEW OF MICRO FINANCE"*

It is indeed a privilege to Chair this Special Session of the National Seminar on MICRO FINANCE.

I have heard with avid delight and great interest, the views and deep insight expressed by each of our respected guests seated on the dais.

The vast wisdom and experience of these eloquent speakers has been amply evident in their speeches and I sincerely thank them for the same.

They have indeed given us a MACRO FOCUS ON MICRO FINANCE.

Our Subject for this Session Today:

"Micro Finance: Practice and Lessons for the Future".

After having heard from experts on the subject, it will now only be my humble endeavour to share with you a brief overview of the subject and highlight a few of its salient features which will have an impact on its future.

To begin with, what is Micro Finance?

---

* (Mr.Shariar Karim is a senior corporate trainer with 30 years' of experience in AIR INDIA)

Micro Finance is a simple but powerful tool that enables the poor to pull themselves out of poverty. Most commonly, it involves making small loans to the working poor in developing countries. These loans are usually less than $200 and are made by local organizations called micro finance institutions. The loans are used by the working poor to establish or expand small businesses that generate additional income for the family. This extra income allows a poor family to buy food, access healthcare, educate their children, put aside savings and lay the foundation for a better future.

Micro finance has emerged as an effective poverty alleviation tool because it is based on the fundamental principle that human beings are motivated to do whatever it takes to make themselves as well off as possible.

Consider the story of Puja Patel, a single mother who lives with her four children in a village in India. With a $50 loan, she bought a sewing machine. She made clothes, sold them for a profit, and repaid the loan with interest. She was also able to save some money to buy books and send her children to the local school. This is micro finance in action.

Small Loans. Big Impact.

Can a $50 loan really make a significant impact on a person's life?

Absolutely!

While $50 may seem small, it is important to remember that the working poor typically live on less than $2 a day. To them, a $50 loan is roughly equivalent to an entire months' income. With that extra income, they can buy supplies or equipment that can help them start new businesses or earn more income from their existing businesses.

Even a small increase in income can make a difference in their lives. First and foremost, extra income can help a poor family meet basic needs: rice and vegetables for a daily meal, kerosene for cooking, or mosquito nets to prevent disease. Hopefully, receiving a first loan is often only the beginning of an ongoing process. Successful loan repayment allows borrowers to take out additional, and often larger, loans. This helps them expand their income even further over time.

A steady and increasing source of income, however small, reduces a poor family's vulnerability to the vagaries of their precarious existence. They can often begin to save money for the first time, providing a financial safety net against unexpected problems. Savings also allow them to access new comforts and services that can improve their living conditions.

For example, a mother might be able to afford to let her children go to school instead of sending them off to beg in the streets or work in the fields. Or it might allow a family to save enough to replace their plastic roof with one made of tin, or fix a long-broken window.

In this way, the small sum of $50 could be the difference for a poor woman between destitution and a secure future for herself and her family. It can empower her to do things that women in her society were never able to do, like serve in the local government, giving her a sense of pride, achievement and dignity. It can provide security and hope, allowing her to fulfill her dream that her children will live a better life than she could have ever imagined for herself.

Basically, this is what Micro finance is all about.

The origin of this concept can actually be traced as far back to the mid 19th century. It has been evolving since then and has gained prominence and global recognition with this story that took place not that long ago and at a place not very far from here.

It can be called the Beginning of the Micro Finance Movement.

In 1974, famine struck Bangladesh. At the time, Dr. Muhammad Yunus was a professor of economics at the University of Chittagong.

It is generally said that an Economist is one who will tell you tomorrow why what he predicated yesterday did not come true today. But not Dr.Yunus , he was an economist with a difference.

Disillusioned by the elegant theories of economics that could not explain the thousands of poor people dying of starvation on the streets, he was determined to find a practical way to help the poor. During a visit to the nearby village of Jorba, he was astounded to find that a sum of $27 could radically change the lives of 42 people in the village. This was the sum of money they collectively needed to buy bamboo to make the stools they sold to make a living. He took $27 from his pocket and made 42 loans to the stool makers in this tiny village. They were able to pay him back with interest and take a step towards lifting themselves out of poverty.

This simple idea that the poor could use credit to lift themselves out of poverty, led Dr. Yunus to create The Grameen Rural Bank in 1983. Since its inception, it has made over $8.96 billion in loans to over eight million borrowers. Its methodologies have become the cornerstone of the micro finance industry.

In 2006, The Grameen Bank and Dr. Yunus were awarded the Nobel Peace Prize.

Explosive Growth

In the 1970s and 80s, inspired by Grameen's success, social innovators and organizations around the world began to experiment with different programmes to bring financial services to the poor. Micro finance institutions proved that it was actually possible to build viable businesses through lending to the poor. The number of micro finance institutions increased rapidly.

And so, Micro finance gradually developed to be a worldwide movement, no longer being a subject matter of micro finance practitioners alone.

Governments, donors, development agencies, banks, foundations, corporations, business communities, civil societies, researchers, universities, consultants, philanthropists and others began taking an increasing interest in it.

The increasing level of acceptance of micro finance among the various groups of stakeholders worldwide presented the following questions:

Is micro finance (MF) becoming popular because it is a good business to make money?

Or

Is it because MF is a powerful tool to fight poverty?

Or

Is it because of both?

Kofi A. Anan, the US Secretary General answers in the following words:

"Since, the concept was born in Bangladesh almost three decades ago, micro finance has proved its value, in many countries, as a weapon against poverty and hunger. It really can change people's lives for the better, especially the lives of those who need it most."

This statement by Kofi A. Anan, the UN Secretary General, succinctly validat the effectiveness of micro finance as a weapon to eradicate poverty. It has bee evidenced worldwide that micro finance helps the poor to overcome poverty, and not through charity. It is a financial system that serves the poor with financial services in a most effective and productive way.

The 2006 Micro Finance Summit Campaign Report estimates that there are now more than 3,000 micro finance institutions, serving more than 100 million poor people in developing countries. The total cash turnover of these institutions worldwide is estimated at $2.5 billion and the potential for new growth is outstanding.

Micro Finance goes Mainstream

In the early years of micro finance, most organizations lending to the poor were funded by private or government grants. In the 1990s, it became apparent that micro finance institutions would be unable to sustain their rapid growth rates if they depended solely on grants for funding. Many micro finance institutions started to restructure their operations to make themselves attractive to investors.

In recent years, many institutional and high net worth investors have begun to invest in micro finance. Attracted by the high growth rates, funds focused on lending to micro finance institutions were created. Today, major banks such as Morgan Stanley, Deutsche Bank and Citigroup have begun to offer products and services that enable investments in micro finance.

With MicroPlace, investment in micro finance truly goes mainstream. Everyday people now have the opportunity to participate in this new industry by purchasing investments that earn a financial return while making a positive social impact on the world.

LESSONS FOR THE FUTURE

Can Commercial Banks do Micro Finance?

It is desirable and indeed essential that commercial banks should be involved in micro finance. If they are not, any impact that micro finance can have on global poverty will be negligible, for it is the privately owned commercial banks which dominate the financial markets in most countries.

Currently, micro finance is being commercialized, but this still mostly involves MFIs becoming commercial banks — or the setting up of commercial banks doing only micro finance. It is observed that most of the commercial banks that have moved into micro finance are state banks.

Cases of preexisting, privately owned commercial banks 'downscaling' and starting micro finance operations are still relatively few and far between.

Although there are success stories — examples include Hatton National Commercial Bank in Sri Lanka, and a number of private banks in India through a programme started by the National Bank of Agriculture and Rural Development (NABARD).

Many of the commercial banks that have tried to downscale have faced considerable problems, and have not achieved impressive levels of outreach.

If micro finance is truly to 'take off' globally, such that it is no longer dependent on donors, and no longer equated with 'development interventions', then this situation must change.

There are many reasons why privately owned commercial banks are put off entering the micro finance market, despite its apparent potential profitability, and why those banks that have 'taken the plunge' have in many cases faced problems. Commercial banks are answerable to their shareholders, who live and die by the bottom line and demand maximum returns. Most do not feel that micro finance will guarantee them this.

Standards and regulatory requirements with which commercial banks have to comply, particularly regarding unsecured lending, and interest rates, are inappropriate for micro finance operations.

The organizational structures, procedures, products and methodologies of commercial banks are not suited to micro finance, and changing them can be difficult, time-consuming and expensive.

There are also significant cultural barriers to be overcome; staff and managers of commercial banks often still perceive the poor as unbankable, and the ways of working required to reach out to them as unbecoming for professional business people like themselves.

These perceptions have not been helped by bad experiences in the past with government and donor led attempts to induce commercial banks to lend to the poor through mechanisms such as compulsory targeting and provision of low cost funds for onlending.

Nonetheless, commercial banks also have a number of competitive advantages as compared to other players in micro finance. They have the necessary management expertise, systems and physical infrastructure in place, are able to accept deposits and have access to other sources of funds such as equity capital.

Capacity Building

For healthy growth of MFIs and for meeting the challenges of micro finance expansion, it is necessary that the training facilities be extended and training materials be updated and upgraded.

Legal and Regulatory Environment

An enabling legal and regulatory environment is important for the development of the micro finance industry and its integration with the mainstream financial sector. This is an area where the government has a vital role to play.

Mobility of Funds and Personnel

For developing sustainable micro finance programmes in different countries, it is necessary that there should be easy and rapid mobility of financial and human resources across the regions and the countries.

Interest Rate

Interest is the main source of income for MFIs. Their sustainability and profitability depend on their interest income. Some argue that it should be enough to cover the cost of operation and allow some profit for capitalization but it should not be so high that it appears exploitative.

Taxation

There is a controversy whether micro finance institutions should pay taxes and what should be the taxation policy for micro finance.

Should the micro finance sector as a whole enjoy a tax holiday and remain outside the tax net?

These are the issues that should be taken care of by the regulatory authorities in order to create a tension free environment for micro finance development.

Conclusion

In conclusion, it may be said that — Micro finance has come a long way despite doubts expressed and criticism launched about its viability, impact, and poverty fighting capacity. The pioneers in the field and the practitioners at large with their commitment, determination, and innovations have not only demonstrated its power and success, but also accelerated its growth.

The Micro credit Summit Campaign deserves credit for making it a worldwide movement. Everyone who has supported or participated in this movement deserves high appreciation.

There should, however, be no room for complacency. The task of building a poverty-free world is yet to be finished. There are still over 1.2 billion people living in extreme poverty on this planet. They are not living in one country or region but are spread all over the world.

I am reminded here of the dream of Mahatma Gandhi as recalled by Pandit Jawaharlal Nehru — "The ambition of the greatest man of our generation has been to wipe every tear from every eye. So long there are tears of suffering so long our work will not be over."

And so as Robert Frost said "there are promises to keep and miles to go before we sleep, and miles to go before we sleep........."

Thank you.

■■■

8

Micro Finance: Some Basics

Mr. Abhishek Chokshi
Vice President,
Matrix Financial Consultants Ltd.

The Case for MFIs*

Let me start with a pretty simple example, if you travel in an aeroplane, at the start, before the journey, the air hostess announces that you should be taking care of these things, and when you go up in the air, sometimes what happens is the air pressure is very low, so the oxygen mask comes out of the upper body and you have to wear that mask — so whenever air hostess announces that, she says that first you have to wear a mask and then you have to wear mask. So why does she say that? Because when you are in the need of contingency, first you have to save yourself then you can help others and save others. So in the case of micro finance, the people who say that micro finance industry should not be doing any profits, or should be doing very less amount of profit, or not-for-profit organizations. They should understand that, if the micro finance company itself is not proper or stable, then how can they help other people to come up in their life? That's why profits — commercial viability in any micro finance company is very-very necessary. So I agree that it should not be exorbitant rates, like very-very high rates, should not be charged. But reasonable profit, should be there. One more reason that why micro finance company's rate is very high, is because cost of operation is very high, as Mr. Anil Jadhav, who is the MD of a micro finance company itself explained to us, that the main cost of funds from the banks, which is about 12-13%, and then the

* (Text of the speech delivered by Mr.Abhishek Choshi, Senior Associate, Matrix Financial Consultants, Lower Paqrel, Mumbai)

cost of operation is about 7 to 8%, of any micro finance company. So total cost comes to 20%. So how do you expect that every micro finance company will survive, if they will be charging less than 20%, it is not possible. So that is why the higher rates are there. Second thing, you being a student, you may not be aware about the flat rate system. So let me explain to you, what flat rate means, if I take a loan of Rs. 10,000, at flat rate of 15%, for example, so I have to pay overall interest of Rs. 1500, so 10,000 ×1500, and so Rs. 11,500 is divided into 52 week installments. At least you must be aware that how the micro finance functions, there is a weekly repayment, and all of you know all that. So Rs. 11,500 is divided by 52 weeks.

But generally when a bank gives a loan, if banks' interest rate is 15%, then it is on reducing balance manner, so if you are paying weekly, so the interest is charged only on the balance which is left to be paid, so that is how micro finance interest rates, and bank interest rates are different. So if micro finance is charging 15% flat interest rate, that means it is 30% reducing balance interest rate, it is double of the banks' rate. Now are you clear of that concept?

Second thing, you students may not be aware — but your mind must be asking this question, that why this debt is required? Why do I go to bank, if I have let's say Rs. 5 crore of equity on micro finance company?

Audience Member: There is interest benefit.

Mr. Abhishek Chokshi: Can you elaborate?

Mr. Abhishek Chokshi: No, but why should I take loan if I have my own money? Why should I add on more and more equity. Let's see if I have a 5 crore equity value, and if the demand from the micro finance borrowers is, let's say Rs. 15 crores, why should I take more of debt.

Audience Members: Tax benefits.

Mr. Abhishek Chokshi: Theoretically, it is true, but practically what happens is, let's say cost of — have you studied this concept, cost of capital? So, cost of equity capital is always high, and cost of debt is always low, so let's say if I have Rs. 5 crore of my own money, and let's say if I need 10% more equity and that amount earning interest, let's say about 30%, right? So, 15 × 30, so it is Rs. 4.5 crore, and that Rs. 4.5 crore, you have to disburse among the equity players, right. But if I take a loan of Rs. 10 crores, then I only have to pay the 12% interest rate. So what happens is the — when you are paying 18%, (30 minus 12), 18%, straight goes to the equity players.

So let's say, for example, Rs. 5 crores is equity, Rs. 10 crores is settled. So, I will be earning Rs.4.5 crore from your micro borrowers, on that Rs. 10 crore, let's say if I am paying 12% on the bank loan, so Rs. 1.2 crore I will be paying to the bankers, so remaining Rs. 3.3 crore is the profit. So that Rs. 3.3 crore profit is on Rs. 5 crore of equity. In the previous case, Rs. 4.5 crore profit was on Rs.15 crore of equity. So did you understand? So, adequate capital should be there, so that there is no default problems.

So since all my points have been covered by the other speakers, what I will try to do is; I will try to tell you about other opportunities, apart from micro finance. One, very-very big opportunity which is going to be growing in India in next few years is affordable housing. You must be reading a lot about affordable housing in newspapers. So, I am a bit drifting from the micro finance subject, but it is linked to the poor people, that's why I am taking that subject with me. So in affordable housing, what happens is, typically, what builders used to do, they used to treat their buildings as real estate, so as an asset; but these days, since there is lack of space in cities like Bombay, and real estate prices are very high, people have come to the concept of affordable housing. So what happens is, the builder treats a building as a factory product, so what he does is, they have such processes, by which they manufacture houses as if they have been manufactured in a factory. So what happens in a factory, the cost of making one thing, as I make number of products, the cost of making one things is very low, constantly becomes low. So in affordable housing, they make such processes, by which if you make, let's say 10 houses, the cost is X, but if you make 100 houses, the cost is not 10 times, it is a bit less. So, these are some of the techniques used by affordable housing builders, so that people can afford very cheap houses, and do you know what are the prices of such affordable housing? Let's say if you want to buy a 1BHK flat in Vashi, how much does it cost to you? Approximately, Rs. 30-35 lakh? Such affordable houses are one-room kitchen houses, and they cost you about Rs. 5 to Rs. 6 lakh, can you believe that? It is Rs. 5 to Rs. 6 lakh. So, it is so much affordable for poor people, and with this affordable housing, there is another opportunity, which many micro finance companies are tapping, which is affordable housing finance. So, they do financing to the people who buy their affordable houses. So, this is one more opportunity which is coming up in a very big way in India. There is one consulting firm called as Monitor Consulting, which is doing a great study on this affordable housing opportunity in India. You can go to their website, and you can find various reports on what is this opportunity. The third and not so very famous is school financing companies. There is one company in Hyderabad, which is doing school financing. So for starting of schools, so that opportunity is to approach school financing companies. So, under school financing opportunity, everything related to school are taken up by the school finance companies. So basically, if a child wants to take education, and mind well, if you want to go abroad, if you want to do MBA, then for those purposes, educational loans are available, up to Rs. 4-Rs. 5 lakh. But for school fees, if a poor child wants to go to a school, there is no education finance specially available for that thing. So, people have started finance companies for that also. Then there are finance companies starting for medical financing. So if someone wants to go through an operation — now they have medical insurances also, but in poor — I mean, in rural areas, there is no insurance concept for medical facilities. So, they have started medical finance companies, so I am giving you lots of ideas as to — if you are willing to start your own finance company or if you are willing to join, there are so many options, apart from micro finances, available.

Now, do you know a concept of priority sector in banking? In India, there are many sectors, whose development is very necessary. For example, agriculture is there. Then poor people's development is necessary. So, these are some of the sectors which are of priority to India. So what RBI has done, they have told all the banks that they have to finance to these priority sectors to the extent of 40% of their total loans. So if they are giving Rs. 100 as loans, 40% should at least go to the priority sector. At the end of the year, RBI comes and checks, whether 40% has gone to the priority sector, and micro finance is included in that priority sector. So, banks do lend to micro finance companies more, because it is included in priority sector.

For example, if the professor comes and tells you that your exam is 10 days from now, when will you start studying. Tell me very honestly. Maybe last two-three days, or you will study for all the 10 days. Who will study for all the 10 days? Apart from all these geniuses, most of us will study for last two-three days. It is the similar cases with all the banks. If RBI is telling that you will have to fulfill your priority sector target on the last day of the year, then what do they do is, they give all the loans, mostly in last four to five months of the year. So what happens is, in the first six-seven months, they don't get — they hardly get any loans. So that is why what happens, let's say, if a micro finance company's requirement is let's say Rs. 100 crore over a year's time, what happens is, they get 70-80% of the sanction, sanction means loan sanctions from the banks at the end of the year. So what happens — and they are not able to deploy the whole money at that time. So they are burdened with more interest costs. That is why their interest cost increases; because let's say if you have got money in your account, but you are not able to give it as loans, what happens, you have to pay interest to banks, but you are not getting interest from borrowers, so your interest cost increases. So if RBI, instead of annualizing the priority sector, if they do quarterly target for priority sector, then the loan amount will be equally distributed over the year.

So I mean, are you understanding what I am trying to tell? So what will bankers have to do in that case? Every three months, they will have to pass on the loans to the priority sector, so in that way there will be a cost saving for a micro finance company, the major cost is interest cost, right? They have to take loans from banks, and they have to give loans. So, major cost is interest costs, apart from the infrastructure. So if they can save on those big costs, then they can obviously reduce the interest rate and do what as RBI says.

One more important thing is, there are certain MFIs, who are focusing more on building client relationship by providing them many other services, like medical services, health services, educational services, and some of the MFIs, they are only focused on lending the money, taking back. What will happen in these cases, the MFI which is only focused on lending and recovering, may become a very big company, because they are focused on their activity, but whenever an instance like Kolar happens, the clients will only prefer to payback to those MFIs with whom their relations are very good. Do you know what happened in Kolar? Kolar is a region in Karnataka, and what happened, there were many MFIs lending their amounts in Kolar. So what happened was, the district collector of Kolar, towards that you should not be feeling bad to paying back your money to MFIs, I will take care of all the MFIs, you don't pay back to them, because they are charging very high interest. And in Kolar, not even a single person paid back their money, and there was a mass default. This happened I guess two-three years back, in 2006-07. So this was a very severe concern on micro finance companies for their existence, even some of the banks and most of the banks started saying no to all the micro finance companies, because they didn't want to lend them, because these are — ultimately they are uncollateralized loan, they have no security. So if there is no security, and if such instance happens, then what the MFI is going to do, they are not having any assets backing, they will not be able to sell any asset. So what they are going to do? They will not be able to do anything, and so many MFIs, who were focused in that area, got washed off. And one or two were our clients, who got washed off, their whole portfolio got washed off, because their major concentration was in Kolar. But take my words, Basics was one of the MFIs which was there and all the clients of Basics repaid them, and you tell me why? Because Basics had maintained super client relations. Some MFIs like Basics what do they do is, they literally mentor their clients, they explain to their clients, like Mr. Anil Jadhav was telling right now, they exactly help their clients for coming up in their life. So if all the MFIs does that, then the main mission for which the MFI was started, will be fulfilled, otherwise as they say, they will be glorified moneylenders, nothing else. And one more thing, what happens if — we talk about it 70-75% of Indian population is poor, and whenever micro finance company starts, they prepare some introductory document, that what exactly the micro finance company is and what are their plans. Everyone writes that we are planning to target the 70% of Indian poor, who are in poverty, we will finance them, we will help them to come up in the life. But just imagine, if the interest rates are so high, let's say if the interest rates are, to be conservative, 30%, right. If the interest rates are 30% and 70% of the population is going to get money at 30%, then what will be the return on equity of the whole country? I mean, is it possible? See, right now our country is growing at 8-9%, and the world is saying that wow, it is such a great growth rate. If at that time, once, all the members of India are covered by all the MFIs. And see it is not possible for a country to grow at such high rate. So what will happen, defaults will happen. So that is the reason, RBI has come out with certain guidelines that will reduce our interest rates, otherwise it will be a problem. So, you have to understand this logic, that why RBI is saying no to change such high interest rates; RBI is saying let's control our interest rate, because poor people will not be able to sustain such high interest rates. But not to say on the other side, whoever wants to start their own MFIs, this is really the best time to start, because MFIs are so much in focus, people are willing to invest in them, banks are willing to lend money to them. And there are so many unexplored areas in India. The southern areas are full, but believe me, the studies say that only 40% to 50% of the areas have benefitted in south also. In North, West, East and the Central part of the country, there are so many unexplored areas for MFIs. So if you want to start an MFI, just go find a region where there is very less penetration, just set up your brands, do some study and you will definitely be successful in starting an MFI; because India is having so many poor people to be served yet and you know there is a lot of scope.

Just to give an example, see what we do about syndication for micro finance companies and many other companies. Debt syndication means, physically we arrange loans from banks and from other institutions to the companies. So what happens is currently, the only lenders to MFIs are banks and some of the developmental institutions. Developmental institutions means basically some finance companies. But there are so many other sources like mutual fund, insurance companies, provident fund companies, they have not yet financed the micro finance companies. There are only two or three transactions which has happened with mutual fund industry, and the whole mutual fund industry is yet to be tapped by micro finance companies. So, there is so much of money yet to be involved in micro finance, that we — I mean, you know the talks of micro finance companies will go bust and micro finance companies will not survive, I really laugh at that. Secondly, there are talks that micro finance companies are, you know, it's a bubble and they are the next subprime, but if you notice very carefully, what was subprime crisis, the subprime crisis, the borrowers in the subprime crisis, were people with bad credit history. But in micro finance, it is not necessary that all the borrowers will be having bad credit. They don't have any credit history. I mean, see, the people in the micro finance industry are so poor, that they don't have any credit history, so who are we to judge that they will be bad or they will be good. So, there is no subprime crisis, when we count in micro finance. If you ask me what is going to happen in micro finance companies in next 10-15 years, according to me, many-many small micro finance companies were not able to grow, they will do mergers and acquisitions with the bigger or mid-size ones. Currently, who are mid-size and small size, but very-very efficient, they are going to grow to a larger player, like SKS and — and the larger ones, maybe probably after 10-15 years, I see that they may become a bank or something like that, and most importantly, I see that major poor population of India standing on their feet respectively, earning properly and living a very-very good life.

Some are lending them, so some investor groups found that nobody is lending to these people who are having bad — see bad credit history means what, that means they must have defaulted in their past or something like that, that is called as bad credit history. So with such history, and intentionally defaulted, not unintentionally. So such people, to them they started lending money for buying houses, right, at higher rates, because there are some prime. See, prime means what, they are proper customers, they are having good credit history. Subprime means, they are below it. So they started charging higher interest rates and they sold them houses, etcetera. So now, as the house prices started increasing, so they will have defined loan of 1 lakh and I want that house, now the price is 2 lakh, right, if the house price increases then there is no problem, because collateral security is there. But if house price starts decreasing, then let's say for example, if you are a bad customer, right, and if you have taken 1 lakh of loan and your house price is now 50,000, will you repay if you are a bad customer? No obviously, you will sell off the house and you will just run away, because instead of 1 lakh, your house value is only 50,000. (inaudible) 1 lakh back to the bank. Right. So that is why the subprime crisis happened, and in micro finance is absolutely underrated. I mean, there is — the people are trying to remove these poor people from their poverty, people are trying to do decent good things, people are trying to educate them. They are trying to take care of your health, right. So, the micro finance companies are helping those people. If someone helps you, will you do bad with me? Unless it's an extreme case — in normal cases, you will not do the right, and —

Audience Member: But we can say that there are some chances in the near future, because we can't find a new customer everytime.

Mr. Abhishek Chokshi: No, see still right now Indian market is — there are 83 crore poor people in India, and the micro finance company have hardly touched any people, they have hardly touched 10%-15% of the market, there is still gap to be covered.

Audience Member: So we can say that in future, there are other chances for subprime crisis?

Mr. Abhishek Chokshi: No, see subprime crisis is very-very different, that is what I am trying to explain you. Subprime crisis happens when a collective mass of people say no, that we won't pay to the — because their security value is less than their loan value, but here there is no security only na. This is not subprime. And these incidences does not happen for 83 crore people at a time yaar. These incidences happen in something like Kolar. Like Kolar is an example, even if it was a political mischief, so some things happened here and there, but it does not happen in whole country, something like this.

Unidentified Speaker: I can add on something, subprime is not only about customer, subprime customer's intention is not right, asset is not right, his project is not right, so everything is not right. Here in micro finance, the purpose is right, focus on the purpose, purpose is survive, so customer survive. Even, let"s say hardly one or 2% are intentional defaulter, but still there are other people who will force them, they should not default. Purpose always there, not to — it is prime purpose, Kirana stuff, not functioning, house will not function. So he will not — but his will, Cow, buffalo, agriculture, all are prime activities and that's why it won't become subprime.

Thank you.

■■■

9 Malegam Subcommittee: Need for Microinspection and Regulation

Prof. Raghavendra S. Bendigeri

In the recent past, Micro finance institutions have been making news for all the wrong reasons. Conceptualized to uplift the downtrodden, the model initially seemed to be highly successful. However, ambition and avarice on part of Micro finance institutions have contaminated the intent and functions of these institutions. Companies such as SKS and Spandana Spoorty raised easy finance in the name of the poor, however reaped most of the gains themselves. Thus, poor shareholders have been deprived of wealth that should have rightfully been theirs.

It all started around 1999 when MFIs were doing microlending as charitable organizations or NGOs. The promoters saw tremendous business opportunity and potential, but their non-corporate identity stunted their growth. Commercial investors were not interested in buying equity because profits cannot be extracted out of an NGO. Banks were not keen to lend money because an NGO's assets cannot be attached and identified easily. So, MFIs decided to metamorphose into for-profit organizations.

These organizations had a number of options but the option that was most suitable to their goals and objectives was to transform into a non-banking finance company (NBFC). This also made community ownership a stated objective. But the double-faced relationship and hypocrisy of these promoters have brought a novel and noble concept to disrepute.

Lack of regulation, transparency and gradual permeation of malpractices into the industry have forced the Government to intervene.

As a result, the Reserve Bank of India in October 2010 set up a Subcommittee of its Central. Board of Directors to study the issues and concerns in micro finance sector, under the Chairmanship of Shri. Y.H. Malegam, a senior member on the Reserve Bank's Central Board of Directors. Other members of the Subcommittee included Shri Kumar Mangalam Birla, Dr. K.C. Chakrabarty, Deputy Governor, Smt. Shashi Rajagopalan and Prof. U.R. Rao. Shri V.K. Sharma, Executive Director, Reserve Bank of India was the Member Secretary to the Subcommittee.

The committee which submitted its report in January 2011 has thrown a lot of light on nature, overall functioning and structure of Micro finance as it exists currently.

The committee has made a number of recommendations to reform the nature of this sector to make it more transparent.

These recommendations have been summarized below:

The first recommendation pertains to NBFCs. The committee has recommended creation of a separate category of NBFCs, which will be designated as NBFC-MFIs.

The committee has listed major criteria which an organization should fulfill in order to qualify as NBFC-MFI.

The committee states that:

- NBFC should be "a company which provides financial services predominantly to low-income borrowers, with loans of small amounts, for short-term, on unsecured basis, mainly for income-generating activities, with repayment schedules which are more frequent than those normally stipulated by commercial banks" and which further satisfies the regulations specified in that behalf.
- The subcommittee has come up with some additional qualifications if an NBFC wants itself to be classified as NBFC-MFI. These are:
  - The NBFC-MFI should hold at least 90% of all assets (other than cash and bank balances and money market instruments) in the form of qualifying assets.

- The annual family income of borrowers should not exceed Rs. 50,000.
- A ceiling of Rs. 25,000 has been imposed on the loan that can be availed by a single borrower.
- At least 75% of the loans given by the MFI should be for the purpose of income generation.
- The other services that an MFI provides or intends to provide should be in accordance with the type of service and the maximum percentage of total income as prescribed.

❖ The subcommittee has recommended that organizations which qualify as NBFC-MFIs will be given loans on a priority basis by the banks and thus will be entitled to "Priority Status". Also with respect to interest chargeable, there should be an average margin ceiling of 10% for MFIs which possess a loan portfolio of Rs. 100 crore and 12% for smaller MFIs and 24% for individual loans.

In order to make the process more transparent, the Committee has recommended the levy of only three types of fees namely:

(a) processing fee,

(b) interest, and

(c) insurance charge.

Some other major issues of concern are multiple lending, over borrowing, ghost borrowers and recovery by unfair and coercive means.

The recommendations pertaining to mitigation of these are:

❖ Limitation of membership of the borrower with respect to SHG or JLG to one.

❖ Borrower cannot borrow from more than two MFIs.

❖ A minimum window period between the disbursement of loan and the commencement of recovery.

❖ Tenure of the loan cannot be fixed for all loans. They should vary with the amount.

❖ Establishment of a Credit Information Bureau.

- Responsibility for avoidance of coercive methods of recovery lies with MFI and its Management.
- The Committee has also recommended that the RBI must prepare a draft Customer Protection Code that should be compulsorily adopted by all MFIs.
- Constitution and Enforcement of grievance redressal procedures and establishment of ombudsmen.

For monitoring compliance with regulations, the Subcommittee has proposed a four-pillar approach with the responsibility being shared by:

(a) MFI,

(b) Industry Associations,

(c) Banks, and

(d) The Reserve Bank.

Micro Finance (Development and Regulation) Bill 2010

While reviewing the proposed Micro Finance (Development and Regulation) Bill 2010, the Subcommittee has recommended that entities governed by the proposed Act should not be allowed to do business of providing thrift services. It has also suggested that NBFC-MFls should be exempted from the State Money Lending Acts and also that if the recommendations of the Subcommittee are accepted; the need for the Andhra Pradesh Micro Finance Institutions (Regulation of Money Lending) Act will not survive.

The Subcommittee has cautioned that while recognizing the need to protect borrowers, it is also necessary to recognize that if the recovery culture is adversely affected and the free flow of funds in the system interrupted, the ultimate sufferer will be the borrowers themselves as the flow of fresh funds to the micro finance sector will inevitably be reduced.

Case Studies

1 Bank of India's Approach to Micro Finance

Mr. N.C. Kulbe, GM, Priority Sector,
Bank of India

Respected Dr. Abha Pethe, Director Department of Economics, University of Mumbai, Dr. N.A. Mujumdar, Former Principal Advisor, RBI, Mr. Tiwari, Dr. Sreedharan, Director, Oriental Institute of Management, my colleagues from the banks, respected faculty members, and dear students.

Let me talk about micro finance. We are associated with the poor, poor of the country, and when we talk of the poor and micro finance, how can we forget Nobel Laureate Mohammad Yunus from Bangladesh, who is the founder father of this movement of micro finance. The poor is lying on one side, who has been planted in a pond, instead of the field.

"Garib aadmi un gonsai(?) paudhon ki tarah hai, jinko ek damde mein laga deta hai. To agar unko bhi wahi jameen, puri opportunities kehne ka matlab ye hai, agar milti, to who bhi anya pedon ki tarah bahut lambi, falduar vruksh ban jaate." So that kind of a restriction is there to the poor also. They have all the capabilities for them grow economically in a big way. It is rightly said by Dr. Shirahatti that the banking channels has also not been able to reach them.

If you remember, (those who are really studying financial inclusion), in 2008, a report by Rangarajan Committee has been there, which states clearly that, only 40% of the people of the country has an account with any banking system, or financial institutions, or post offices also included, and there are 60% who do not have an account. Therefore, this in fact is the reality. But, things are changing, and changing very fast and changing for the better. However, right now, if they are not having a bank account, what to talk about credit to them. It is not only prevalent in the rural areas.

What happens to those very people who move to urban areas, they do not have any identity. They live in some chawl, maybe below the bridge, maybe on the pavement, without any address. Urban poverty is increasing. But still, rural poor maybe more in numbers, but the problems of urban poor are also very much there as far as having a bank account is considered.

Here also, even when there is — in a city like Bombay, I remember 30 years back what kind of thing can happen and you can imagine. A vegetable wholesaler gives some help to a vendor who sells on the streets vegetables. Rs. 100 is given every day, for stocking of vegetables to be sold in the streets. And at the end of the day, in the evening, he has to pay Rs. 110 back. And this goes on forever. This is the highest rate of interest, anywhere in the world charged, for any transaction, because it is 3650%. It's 10% per day, which is per annum, 3650%. Still, both of them are happy, i.e., lender and borrower. That brings us to the role of micro finance institutions. They will not be charging this usurious rate of interest, like moneylender in the village.

Coming to MFIs now, they are the one who are having now thousands of crores of business today, through this — by giving micro finance to these poor people. They charge loan on paper at 15%, but the net effect of that rate of interest is something like 28% to 30%. Problem is, suppose Rs. 10,000 loan is given for two years, that is if it is 15% as I said, he has to pay Rs.13,000. So, this is loaded upfront, added upfront, Rs.13,000 for the next two years, has to be paid every week or every 15 days or every month, without any advantage of this credits. So, it is upfront calculation on Rs. 10,000 for rest of the two years, and not on daily balance reducing basis as prevalent in banks, including Bank of India.

So there again, they end up paying usurious interest or high rate of interest. Government has been trying to bring in some checks for these MFIs, so that they don't charge this. Banks would insure that these MFIs, when we finance them, should not charge high rates of interest, and they should not be charging interest rates of more than 24%. They are telling us then "we are charging 15%, but that is 24, 28, 30%". That makes a difference. Now, the basic question, being a banker, why the banks have not been able to stipulate. This is being exploited by the MFI.

Obvious question would be, such a big bank industry, which has done good work in many areas, why they have not been able to regulate. I am telling you, for the banking industry in fact. I will tell you one small figure that is given by NABARD for last year. They were given a target of Rs. 3,25,000 crore of disbursement for agricultural activities in the country to the farmers for whole of the year. What was their performance, against this target of Rs. 3,25,000 crore, they made disbursement of 3,66,000 crore. The problem does not lie in the requirement of giving them adequate credit. But there are many other advantages, other things which are required to be done by other institutions, as and when you really go into it. But let me now further elaborate on that, and come to another theory. As I said, we are talking about the future of micro finance. What will be the future credit?. Let me tell you that already MFIs are coming in a big way, they are moving from strength to strength. But if we talk about the future, it is going to be again the banks who are going to lead the way for financial inclusion and lending for micro finance is working well. So, as I said, Dr. Shrihatti said that banking has not been able to reach people, that's true.

But after this, Dr. Rangarajan Committee Report came, it was decided that now banks will be doing it through a different system. The problem so far, in this country is, 70% of them some live in rural areas or in rural areas, and this is a big geographical aspect. To reach them, is very difficult first, but to really give the message to them, is also very difficult, in the sense that they are the people who are — most of them are illiterate. Most of them are fatalists, because they live on the vagaries of the nature. Therefore, bankers, if they come forward there is this issue, *"arre bank ka karja vapis karne ki kya jarurat hai, sarkar maaf kardegi."* That heads to the problem, because they do not understand that this is a path which is going to be destructive for them. Banking has spread in the country, but it is not sufficient enough to reach all. So how the banks are going to improve? Some of you might be knowing that, there is a concept of banking correspondent now in this country, where the farmer or the rural poor will not have to walk to the branch. Through BC (Banking Correspondent), they will get the benefit of bank. Initially, Rs. 73,000 of those villages which are having population of more than 2,000 and which are given to one bank. The country has 6,38,000 villages. Out of this, some 5,95,000 are villages to be served by banking industry. But there is a way. It will be done through a banking correspondent.

Let me tell you for Bank of India. Out of these 73,000 villages, we are going to have roughly 3,500 villages, to be served through TCS, HCL, Integraft. These are vendors who will be operating Pan India and they will be taking this banking correspondent's role. They will be at the village itself through a handheld machine. With handheld devices for the smart card operations, they will be transacting cash, for instance, suppose Rs. 20, Rs. 500, Rs. 200. They will be depositing it in the account with the BC, on online, real time, if connectivity is there, credited in their bank account, where it has a nearby branch. And this smart card has been — yesterday (23/9/2010) only we had a meeting with Government of India, who said that this smart card should be handled to get a Kisan Credit Card, that means loan for buying seeds, fertilizers, and other insecticides and other things for agricultural operations, which would enable for some insurance products. Smart Cards should be enabled for meeting some financial needs and moreover later on to make remittances too. Because, remittances — particularly for the urban poor or urban person is very important in the sense that, I have left my family way back in their village, but I have to remit them money time and again, and again. He has to fall back upon that wholesaler, in whichever trade he is. There what he gets for remitting Rs. 2,000, he pays Rs. 200, Rs. 300, sometimes, Rs. 400.

"jo pasine ki kamai hai, aur channels mein deni padti hai. Fact yeh hai, bankers aaj bhi hamare paas jabse core banking, networking moving bank hai, aise remittance, kyunki agar Jharkand ya Bangal ke kisi gaav mein, Bambai mein woh yaha hai, paisa bhejna chahta hai, to usko hamare yaha kisi bhi branch mein jaa sakta hai,." He can go to any of these branches where he fills the 15 digit number account number of that remote branch where he wants to send the money, he can do it in Bandra or Andheri or any branch there, and it would be credited there only, though it will deposit in this branch. We are doing roughly 3,000 to 4,000 such transactions daily. So, bankers on their part, there is no cost in this, because banks don't charge — up to Rs. 25,000. So, bankers are doing their bit. Everywhere they can.

But now we have again come up with another model, that we are going to do a mobile banking thing, as it will be mobile remittance for them, they don't have people or crowd or branches henceforth, that can be done through a mobile through a mobile telephony. On 3rd June, we made a demonstration in Bombay. So, therefore, those things are being done. As I said, Bank of India is going to have 15,000 BCs operating in the country. When I said that more than 2,000 villages, we are having roughly 3,000 odd villages to cater to micro finance. But in addition to that, I have to take care, in all 40,000 villages of the country would be serviced by Bank of India. So that's how I need 15,000 business correspondents could be arranged for me by TCS, HCL or Integraft. Therefore, if you say in future banks are embarking on unprecedented movement of funds. The whole world is looking at India to see if they can succeed in enabling or really exploiting financial infusion in totality, and it will be kind of a feat that may be emulated by others. I think it was to be launched with lot of fanfare, in a big way, by the Prime Minister or other dignitaries. But the formal launch, I think will now take place in 2011. I am, in fact, member of the Internet Association of this publicity committee also. Undoubtedly, this is going to be a future of micro finance, in a way that again the interest will play the most dominant role in this area again. Though micro finance institutions have done very well so far in this area, and they will also be contributing in a variety of ways. But looking at the strength of the banking system, the only problem of staff is being taken care of by engaging business correspondents. Banks would be a major player in this area now, and you can understand that a village boy is going to get a very good employment out of this, because those BCs, business correspondents, most of the time will be from the local area people, and many lakhs of them looking at the total banking industries, requirement of BCs will be getting employment in their place of residence, which is most important to start, both from villages and urban areas.

At the end when I would like to tell you something about bankers' perspective on the micro finance that is going to be there, you must be wondering what is this kind of thing I have explained here.

I was referred to as being Chairman before coming to Bombay, as General Manager, Bank of India. As Chairman, the bank won accolades for financing rural home system, which are numbered at roughly 28,000 now. It has covered 7 million people.

So you can see yourself, probably if I give some material to you, you will analyze in a different way.

You are all students now; your counterpart in villages, never gets an opportunity to study after 6.30 or 7.30 pm. After that, there is no light for them to study. What kind of circumstances they are living, can only be imagined and the plight of housewife can only be thought of. Kerosene lamp is the source of light which always gives you obnoxious vapours, which are not good for heart, not good for lungs, not good for eyes. Therefore, in most testing circumstances, they are living, but this is another case where there is no power, in fact the story is that the poles and the wires are there for last 10 years, but this was not activated and they never used to get light. The fact is that, in that village, when we gave the solar homelight, I said micro finance is not itself a credit input, it could be an enabler, maybe towards that input, like the solar homelight system.

"And this is in their village at 10 pm, in the night, in solar homelight, a finest embroidery work is being done by a lady. In fact, what you see there is NABARD Chairman, Shri U.C. Sarangi, sweating all along. In that village, at night at 10 pm, the date is also given there, and there he was greatly impressed."

In fact, the bank has won a national award for this in London. Thereafter, we won an India Power Award from Government of India for this initiative.

But I say there are many facets of micro finance, which can not only be by way of credit itself, by way of enabling some activities, this lady says *"sir hamne to apne dadi-nani ke jamane se kabhi dekha nahi ki ham raat mein kabhi kaam kar paye hai, ab ham, 6:30, 7, 8 jab bhi time mile, 4-5 ghante ka backup power hai, to 4-5 ghante tak hum kabhi bhi ye kaam kar sakte hai, aur hamari income kam se kam 4,000 rs per month badh gayi hai, aur woh kehte hai".*

The quoted experience has been a subject of study by Indian Institute of Management at Ahmedabad, and other reputed institutes. I am only bringing a point that through micro finance only, 14,000 to 15,000 solar homelight systems have been given. It is self-liquidating or self-repaying in the sense that, whatever they spend on kerosene, roughly Rs. 250 or Rs. 240 per month is calculated, the EMI, the installment to the bank they pay through that, that means that goes out of their pocket, even if they take it and it is hassle-free, good for health.

In BBC, London has said, that this experiment is not only good for health, it is good for business also. So therefore, micro finance in the system is there for banks to take advantage of and definitely they can.

With this probably, I must thank the institute profusely for giving me an opportunity to put forth bankers' perspective, particularly to micro finance, that is going to be the future.

■■■

2 An Overview of Micro Finance Delivery Models in the City of Mumbai

Dr. Minoo Thomas, Principal[1], SIES College, Sion, Mumbai

"It is important not to lose sight of the basic fact that the reduction of income poverty alone cannot possibly be the ultimate motivation of anti-poverty policy."

– Amartya Sen[2]

Urban poverty in developing countries is typically concentrated in slums and other informal settlements. If nothing is done to check the current trend, the number of people living in dire conditions will rise from one billion today to 1.6 billion by the year 2020. These figures call for a revision of Target 11 of Millennium Development Goal No. 7, which aimed at "significantly improving the lives of at least 100 million slum-dwellers by 2020". If the urban context of poverty is not directly addressed, it would be impossible to achieve the goals. Improving the lives of slum-dwellers helps combat HIV/AIDS, improve environmental sustainability, and address gender inequality.

According to 2001 Census of India, Mumbai is a place where more than half of its inhabitants (54.5%) live in slum areas. Mumbai slum-dwellers form the largest group of people among the metropolitan areas of India. Calcutta which also houses a large number of slum dwellers stands second with 32.48% of its population dwelling in slums. Given the magnitude of this huge slum population, this paper tries to analyze the Institutions involved in empowering the urban poor through provision of

---

1 Paper presented by Dr. Minu Thomas, Principal, SIES College Commerce and Economics, Mumbai.

2 Sourced from Assessment of Micro-Macro Linkages in Poverty Alleviation: South Asia, UNDP, October 2003.

Micro finance in the city of Mumbai and assesses the various micro finance delivery models in the city of Mumbai.

Micro enterprise and micro finance development have emerged as major strategies to combat the twin issues of poverty and unemployment that remains a major threat to the economy. In India, the promotional institutions of micro finance are basically of three types, namely:

- Government.
- Banks.
- NGO.

The Background of the Present Study[3]

The research work was carried out by collecting quantitative data based on interviews with NGO[4] functionaries and women entrepreneurs based in Mumbai. The data was collected[5] from nine NGOs and 81 micro entrepreneurs trained by these NGOs. The secondary document analysis together with the informal interviews of key informants built the foundation on which the empirical research was based. The NGO functionaries were interviewed with the help of a questionnaire to assess their micro enterprise development initiatives in the process of empowering women. During the course of primary data collection from NGOs, it was noticed that:

- The reach of a specific scheme of GOI namely SJSRY[6] was restricted to few areas in Mumbai and in fact this scheme was being implemented through select NGOs in the city of Mumbai.

Rationale of Study

- Micro finance and the SHG movement have brought a much-needed revolution in poverty alleviation programmes.
- Micro enterprise and micro finance development have emerged as major strategies to combat the twin issues of poverty and unemployment that remains a major threat to the economy.

---

3 This paper is a part of doctoral work and minor research project sanctioned by University of Mumbai (co-authored by Mrs. Aarthi Kalyanraman) during the period 2005-2008.

4 Names of NGOs mentioned in Appendix.

5 The data was collected from both primary and secondary sources. Purposive sampling technique was used to select the NGOs working for women in Mumbai.

6 The Swarna Jayanti Shahari Rozgar Yojana (SISRY) is a bank-linked self-employment programmes with two major componenets namely Urban Wage Employment Programme and Urban Self-employment Programme (USEP).

The outline of this paper is as follows:

- Background of present study.
- Objectives of the present study/limitation of study.
- Analysis and Discussion.
- Recommendation and conclusion.

Methodology

- Descriptive study: The research work was carried out by collecting qualitative and quantitative data based on interviews with NGO functionaries, women entrepreneurs and two financial institutions based in Mumbai who catered to the needs of urban poor.
- The data was collected from both primary and secondary sources.
- Purposive sampling technique was used to select the NGOs and financial institutions which are working for women in Mumbai.

Objectives of the Present Study

- To study the various Micro finance models to reach urban poor.
- To study the delivery model.
- To study the enabling environment created by these NGOs/banks to assist graduation of SHG members from Micro Finance to Micro Enterprise development.

Limitations of the Study

- The study is only restricted to Mumbai, and therefore it may not reflect the situation elsewhere in the country.
- The researchers tried to assess the extent of micro finance disbursement and resultant micro enterprise development in Mumbai. However, on account of inability to source the primary data and relevant secondary data from these financial institutions had to extensively refer to secondary sources to study the reach and delivery model of the banks under study.
- Initially, it was decided to interview five micro entrepreneurs from every NGO. However, all the NGOs were not co-operative. The researcher had no choice but to interview the women identified by the NGO functionaries.
- Therefore, it was not possible to conduct hypothesis testing on account of variation in number of respondents, small sample size of NGOs and the

technique of sampling undertaken as purposive and convenience sampling techniques were applied.

Analysis and Discussion

Details of the NGOs

- Only three NGOs were involved in the process of disbursement of micro finance namely AMM, SMS and USVA out of 19 NGOs surveyed.
- Of which, only SMS provided detailed information about their programme and the activities undertaken.

Details of the Banks

- Two banks were selected under this study namely SBI and ICICI Bank. However, only SBI provided access to 4 NGOs to which they have disbursed micro finance in the city of Mumbai.

Part A. Findings of NGOs Surveyed

1. Women beneficiaries covered: As this study aimed at only reaching out to NGOs which provided micro enterprise development option to the beneficiaries, a need was felt to assess the various categories of women covered by the NGOs.

Table 1: Various Categories of Women Covered by the NGOs

Variable	Frequency	Per cent
Destitute women	17	89.5
Abandoned women	15	78.9
Divorced	16	84.2
Widow	15	78.9
Bamboo artisans	1	5.3
General	1	5.3
HIV patients	1	5.3
Mentally challenged children (girls)	1	5.3
School drop-outs	2	10.5

Note: Some organizations identified more than one answer.

It can be observed that 89.5% NGOs reached out to destitute women, 78.9% NGOs reached out to abandoned women, 84.2% reached out to Divorce women and

78.9% reached out to widows. From this analysis, we can make out that the NGOs reach out to the most marginalized section of the society and bring them to the mainstream by providing them vocational training and assistance to set up micro enterprises. Thus, the researcher is of the opinion that NGOs act as a good vehicle to empower the marginalized in the society and this was reiterated when the USEP scheme under SJSRY scheme was implemented in Mumbai with the assistance of various NGOs like Apnalaya, SMS, BECC, REAP, YUVA, Yuvak Prathishtan, SUPPORT and Prerana. In fact, it is worth noting that Prerana NGO works for the rights of sex workers in the red light areas of Mumbai and in order to provide them alternate employment option they have involved these commercial sex workers under the SJSRY scheme.

2. Beneficiary empowerment: This variable was used to assess the whether did the NGOs organize programmes to empower beneficiaries by either providing vocational training or organize activities to enable them to start the micro enterprises. The questionnaire was administered to NGOs of only this type. However, on close examination, it was found that the nature of activities organized varied from organization to organization.

Table 2: Empowerment through Micro Enterprise Development

Nature of Assistance	F	%
Vocational training	18	94.7
Vocational training and Provision of micro finance	2	10.5
Provision of Micro finance and Linkage with Training institute	1	5.3
Vocational training and Linkage with Government's SJSRY Scheme	6	31.6
Only Linkage with MF institution	1	5.3

Note: Some organizations identified more than one answer.

From the above table, we can make out that 94.7% NGOs provided vocational training to the women beneficiaries and only one NGO which did not provide vocational training linked its members' to a Micro finance institution in Mumbai. It was observed that 10.5% NGOs such as AMM and SMS provided Micro finance along with vocational training, 5.3% NGOs, i.e., YUVA provided micro finance through its co-operative credit bank and linked the beneficiaries to training institutes for their micro enterprise training requirements. One NGO (USVA) acted as an intermediary between the beneficiaries and a MFI. Similarly, 31.6% NGOs which provided vocational training as a part of its programme enabled the beneficiaries to get maximum advantage by linking them to USEP under the SJSRY Scheme (through the DWCUA component of the said scheme).

3. Methods/approaches adopted by NGOs to make beneficiaries self-reliant: NGOs undertake a number of programmes to empower their beneficiaries. This variable is an attempt to assess the strategies adopted by these NGOs.

Table 3: Methods Adopted to Make the Beneficiaries Self-reliant

Particulars	Frequency	Per cent
Raising awareness level	15	78.9
Undertaking income generation programmes	18	94.7
Formation of SHGs	11	57.9
Provision of micro finance	4	21.1

Note: Some organizations identified more than one answer.

From the above table, we can make out that 94.7% NGOs stated that they undertook income generation programmes, 78.9% raised the awareness level of beneficiaries to become self-reliant, 57.9% NGOs encouraged the formation of self-help groups and 21.1% NGOs such as AMM, YUVA, CH and SMS provided micro-finance. Apart from the above strategies, some organizations resorted to the following strategies as illustrated in the table below:

Table 4: Other Strategies Adopted by NGOs to Make Beneficiaries Self-reliant

Strategies to make beneficiary self-reliant	F	%
By educating them and providing livelihood training and involve them in empowerment programmes to make them independent, by providing them vocational training • in nursing • Paper products • to provide computer literacy • Management of waste	18	94.7
By providing vocational training and organizing adult literacy programme	1	5.3
Our purpose to bring more women, beneficiaries under women co-operatives	1	5.3
We have tied up with ICICI bank to provide micro finance to needy under the partnership model	1	5.3
We propose to bring more beneficiaries under the bachat ghat and link them under SJSRY scheme	2	10.5

We propose to consolidate our urban women empowerment programme	1	5.3
Formation of Credit Co-operative Bank	2	10.5

Note: Some organizations identified more than one answer.

All answers of similar type were collated.

From the above table, we can infer that NGOs have adopted a number of strategies such as:

1. 94.7% NGOs are involved in provision of livelihood training and involving them in empowerment programmes to make them independent.
2. 10.5% NGOs namely AMM and YUVA have established credit co-operative bank to assist its beneficiaries.

Thus, we can infer that NGOs have adopted a number of approaches to empower their beneficiaries.

4. Implementation of a Specific Scheme of GOI for the Urban Poor: The Swarna Jayanti Shahari Rojgar Yojna (SJSRY) scheme[7] was launched in December 1997. SJSRY seeks to provide gainful employment to the urban poor (living below the urban poverty line) unemployed or underemployed, through setting up of self-employment ventures or provision of wage employment. Inputs under the scheme are delivered through the community structures set up on UBSP[8] pattern and Urban Local Bodies (ULBs). The scheme is funded on a 75:25 basis between the Centre and the States. The scheme was initiated to provide gainful employment to the urban poor by encouraging the setting up of self-employment ventures or provision of wage employment and consists of two components, namely:

(i) The Urban Self-employment Programmes (USEP) and

(ii) The Urban Wage Employment Programme (UWEP).

This study is restricted to assessing the reach of USEP (DWCUA)[9] in the city of Mumbai. The researcher is of the opinion that NGOs act as a good vehicle to empower the marginalized in the society and this was reiterated when the USEP scheme under

---

[7] The Ministry of Urban Development and Poverty Alleviation has the mandate for broad policy formulation and monitoring programmes on urban poverty.

[8] Urban Basic Services Programme.

[9] DWCUA — Development of women and child in urban areas. This scheme is distinguished by the special incentive extended to urban poor women who decide to set up self-employment ventures in a group as opposed to individual enterprises. Group of urban poor women take up an economic activity suited to their skill, training, aptitude, and local conditions.

SJSRY scheme was implemented in Mumbai with the assistance of various NGOs like Apnalaya, SMS, BECC, REAP, YUVA, Yuvak prathishtan, SUPPORT and Prerana.

5. NGOs Implementing Schemes of Government of India: This variable was used to assess the reach of NGO programme *vis-à-vis* the Government programme. The researcher was interested in assessing the reach of a specific self-employment programme namely SJSRY scheme amongst urban poor in Mumbai city.

Table 5: NGOs Implementing Schemes of Government of India

Sr. No.	Scheme	Yes	%	No	%
1	SJSRY SCHEME-USEP	6	31.6	13	68.4
2	PMRY	0	-	0	-
3	TREAD	0	-	0	-
4	STEP	0	-	0	-
5	Any Other				
6.	Sarva Shikshan Abhiyan				
7.	Sanjay Gandhi Niradhar Yojana*	2	10.6	17	89.5

* Apnalaya, both 1 and 2.

SF only 1.

From the table, we can infer that 31.6% NGOs were implementing the SJSRY scheme in collaboration with MCGM/Municipal Corporation and were at different levels of implementation. 10.6% NGOs were also involved in implementing two other programs namely Sarva Shikshan Abhiyan and Sanjay Gandhi Niradhar Yojana.

6. Brief description of SJSRY scheme implemented by NGOs. During collection of data, it was noticed that none of the individual beneficiaries were recipients of benefit of this scheme. It was observed that NGOs encouraged SHG formation and encouraged women in groups to take benefits of the scheme, to ensure greater accountability the members.

Table 6: Organizations Implementing SJSRY Schemes of Government of India

Sr. No.	NGO	Year in which implemented by the NGO	Amount sanctioned	Beneficiaries	
				Type	No. of Groups
1	Apnalaya	2005	81,000	Urban BPL women	4 groups
2	BECC	2004	22,000	Urban slum women	1 group
3	SMS	2003	10,00,000	Waste pickers	100 groups
4	REAP	2003	8,50,000	Urban BPL women	85 groups
5	YUVA	2003	2,64,000	Urban BPL women	22 groups
6	Yuvak Prathishtan#	2006	Not yet	Urban BPL women	1 group

amount not yet received

From the above analysis, we can make out that the programme was implemented from 2003 onwards, depending upon the number of members in the group, the amount sanctioned varied accordingly. The benefit was given to only urban BPL population especially women from these NGOs. Thus, we can say that group entrepreneurship is definitely a better alternative when it comes to reaching out to the beneficiaries. The experience gained by the NGO states that group entrepreneurs can be held more accountable as the group typically grows through all group dynamics before agreeing to be a part of this scheme. It is worth mentioning the successful implementations of SJSRY scheme by two NGOs namely, REAP and SMS. These successful examples can be replicated throughout Mumbai and Maharashtra state to begin with.

7. Problems Encountered in the Process of Implementation of SJSRY Schem

It has been observed that though the scheme came into effect in 1997, the actu disbursements occurred only from 2003. Out of the 19 NGOs surveyed, only 6(31.6%) were recipients under this scheme. It was necessary to verify whether the 31.6% NGOs encountered any problem in the process of implementation and what were the suggested measures to ensure whether the scheme can be implemented in a bett r manner.

Table 7: Problems Encountered in SJSRY Implementation and Suggestions to Improve

NGO	Nature of Activity	Problems Encountered	Suggestions, if any
Apnalaya	Catering.	Procedural delay.	-
BECC	Catering.	Procedural delay and lots of documentation work.	Help in marketing their product.
SMS	Segregation and Recycling of waste.	No major problem.	-
REAP	Phenyl, aggarbaties etc.	Lack of expertise in selling products and inability to sell products on a regular basis.	Support should be provided for marketing the products manufactured by the women. They should be linked to various government departments.
YUVA	Catering.	Procedural delays, constant monitoring and follow-up.	Reduce the procedural delay.
Yuvak Prathishtan	Not yet sanctioned.	Lots of procedural work and documentation. Delay in disbursement of amount sanctioned.	Reduce procedural work and documentation work. Amount sanctioned should be released at the earliest.

From the above table, we can make out that majority of the (66.6%) NGOs did face problems on account of procedural work and documentation. Only one organization stated that they do not have major problem. 2(33.33%) NGOs felt that support should be provided for marketing the products. One NGO felt that procedural delay and delay in disbursement of amount sanctioned should be overcome.

8. Reason for Not Availing the Benefit(s) of Government Programme: Around 77(95.1%) women were not linked to any government scheme. Therefore, a need was felt to assess the reason behind non-availment of benefits of government programme.

Table 8: Reason Behind Non-availment of Benefits of Government Programme

	Frequency	Per cent
Not aware	67	87
Did not want to avail	2	3
Aware but did not want to avail	2	3
Aware but did not avail because of long procedure	6	8
Total	77	100

Thus, it can be observed that out of 77 women who did not avail of any scheme, 67(87%) women said that they were not aware of existence of such a scheme, 6(8%) women said that they were aware but did not want to avail because of long procedure.

Part B — Case Study of Stree Mukti Sanghatan (SMS)

SMS was established as a Women's Liberation Organization[10] in Mumbai, India in 1975. The membership to the organization is not restricted on the lines of caste, class, creed educated uneducated. In fact, this is one of the organizations which encourage cross sector learning for enhancing their programmes. The organization has a team of dedicated staff members and volunteers. The Sanghatana functions on democratic principles and decisions are taken in a general body meeting. Men also are eligible to enroll as members. The office bearers are elected in the executive committee meetings. Depending upon the requirements of its activities, subcommittees are appointed based on democratic principles. To carry out its various operations, it is dependent on donor aid, though earned income sources from sale of publications, earnings from day care center, consultancy fee etc., forms a small part of its earnings. In order to achieve its objectives, SMS has collaborated with a number of organizations such as TISS, BARC, MCGM, All-India Radio, Dasra, KEM Hospital, ALERT India, local, regional, national and international organizations, IPH and Mumbai Police.

Parisar Vikas Programme: This programme was launched in the year 1998 in co-operation with the Municipal Corporation of Greater Mumbai (MCGM). This project covers the **poorest of the poor** in Mumbai and aims at addressing the problem of rag pickers (PARISAR BHAGINI) engaged in the task of cleaning waste and problems of waste management. This programme is a result of a survey conducted about the plight of 2000 waste pickers in different parts of Maharashtra.

---

[10] It caters to the needs of upliftment of women irrespective of class, creed, religion, language and nationality. SMS is involved in ongoing mission of liberating women from economic, social, political, cultural and psychological oppression. It believes that women's liberation is not possible at an individual level, it requires a social and collective struggle at three levels: namely intellectual struggle with oneself, struggle in individual practice and Collective struggle. SMS has undertaken the following main tasks, namely: (a) Theoretical study of women's problems. (b) Making women conscious about their rights. (c) Organizing women to address different problems in their life by assisting them to find solution of their problems. SMS and its cause is noteworthy for one main reason namely: They do not have a one fit for all problems. SMS recognizes the fact that women in different spheres of activity and from different economic groups are quite different. Therefore, they have initiated varied activities and programmes. It functions as a nuclear organization, makes efforts at coordination of women from different strata so as to enable exchange of thoughts and experiences as well as develop an awareness of the existence of common problems faced by all the groups as women. The Sanghatana is a united movement of women and is also involved in extending support to the women's liberation movements at different places.

Under the Parisar Vikas Programme, 200 groups of Parisar Bhaginis have been formed with a group leader. Amongst these, 170 groups have already started working as savings group (Bachat Ghat) having disbursed Rs. 50 lakh for its internal lending till (31st March, 2005). SMS has enabled the groups to receive a grant of Rs. 10,000 per group to start micro enterprise under the SJSRY scheme.

SMS has also established two training centers for training Parisar Bhaginis. The women have been organized and are being trained in environmental entrepreneurship programme which includes skills in biocomposting, vermiculture, organic manure making, gardening, leadership development and formation of co-operatives, etc. They have also been provided assistance for educating their children, formation of saving groups, access to micro credit, healthcare and hygiene, Insurance cover (waste pickers have been covered as special category under Janashree Vima Yojana and Antyodaya Yojana) and literacy skills. SMS also imparts pre-primary education to children of Parisar Bhagini by starting Balwadis (kindergartens) in association with PRATHAM.[11]

As a trainer and facilitator, SMS secured work opportunities for Solid Waste Collection and Treatment in major public and private sector housing colonies and office premises, viz., Tata Power, RBI, BEST, Pfizer, CIDCO, MCGM, BARC, Somaiya, etc. 300 trained Parisar Bhaginis successfully brought near zero-waste status in these colonies, campuses and also in the small housing complexes spread over 13 wards in Mumbai. In last 2 years, the work has spread to Navi Mumbai, Kalyan, Dombivili, Thane and Ambernath.

A special Mother and child health centre was started with the support of assistance received from the CSR Department of L&T Ltd. During the World Social Forum (2004) held in Mumbai, it made a sizeable profit by taking over the contract of collection and disposal of waste. SMS has also undertaken the maintenance contract for Nisarga Ruma (Biomethanation) plant developed by scientist of BARC — Bhabha Atomic Research Center with a capacity of five tonnes of biodegradable waste every day.

SMS and Trained Parisar Bhgini Mandal members are also involved in provide vocational training in management of waste in different Municipal wards of Mumbai. To assist Parisar Bhaginis in their social enterprise activity (environmental

[11] PRATHAM is an organization working for universalization of primary education. This organization was set up by Dr. Madhav Chavan, a Ashoka Fellow.

entrepreneurship), the funding was received from "War on Want"[12], (a organization based in UK) and Dasra.[13] SMS has collaborated with Dasra, as it realized that it did not possess the business acumen (concepts of business planning, inventory control, working capital were not a part of its organization structure) to carry out its social enterprise activity. Dasra enabled SMS to build the sheds for segregation of dry waste and train the staff members in acquiring business acumen. On having collaborated with Dasra as a business advisor, Jyoti Mhapsekar states that "... have taught us to keep accounts and ... build strategies", she further stated that "Prior to this, we lacked any life experience in the development of business schemes. Now, we have confidence."

Impact Assessment of Parisar Vikas Programme: The findings of a survey[14] on qualitative and quantitative improvements in the social, economic, health and educational status of 50 rag picker women employed through the Sanghatana in different parts of Mumbai City, illustrates that the initiative of SMS has brought about a difference in the lives of these women. The women surveyed stated that they have changed their perception to life and felt that the society's perception about them has also changed. They were happy and grateful towards the organization, as they believed that the paradigm shift in their social, educational, health and economic status were due to the untiring efforts and initiatives of the organization. Thus, by undertaking solid waste management programme, it has enabled these Parisar Bhaginis to become an important link in environmental entrepreneurship.

The efforts of SMS have been recognized and appreciated both at national and international levels, noteworthy among them are the consultative status from UN-(ECOSOC)[15] received in June 1999 and the Ashoka Fellowship received from the Ashoka Foundation.

From the representation in Figure 1, we can make out that the model adopted by SMS is an integrated one as SMS has networked and collaborated with a number of organizations both at National and International level to fulfill its mission goals.

---

12 War on Want fights poverty in developing countries in partnership and solidarity with people affected by globalization.

13 Dasra collaborated with SMS because of its previous collaborative relationship with the MCGM, which enabled them to get the land to build the sheds for segregation of dry waste.

14 Study was undertaken by students of Nirmala Niketan Institute of social work in the year 2003-04; the researcher received a copy of the survey from SMS.

15 UN-ECOSOC.

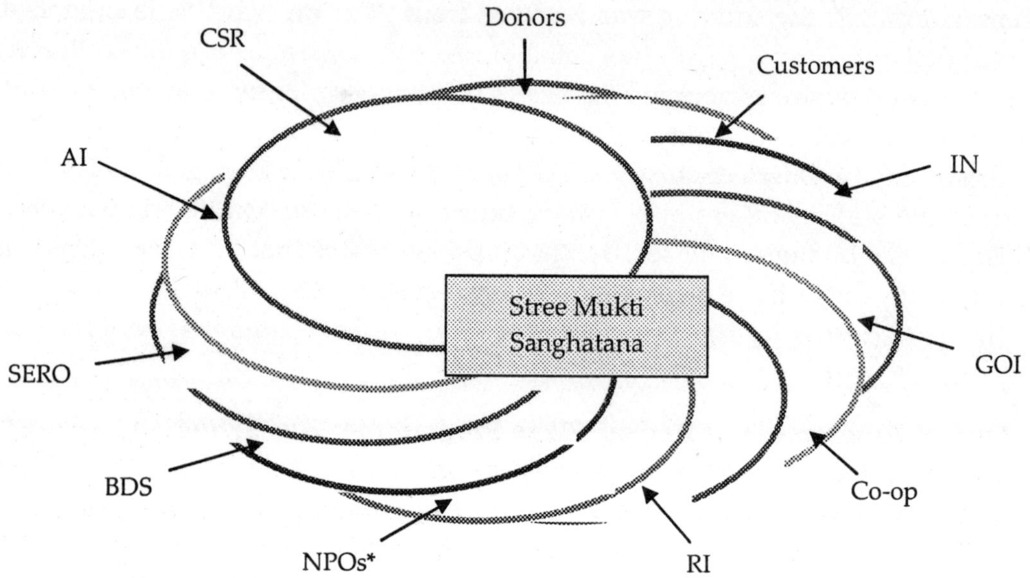

Figure 1: Model of Stree Mukti Sanghatana

Source: Based on field work.

Key for figure 1:

NPOs - Local bodies and NGOs in local, regional national and international level.

IN - UN-ECOSOC, War on Want

GOI - National, state, MCGM, Mumbai Police, BMC Schools.

Academic Institutions – SIESCOMS, TISS

CSR - Telco, BARC, L&T Ltd.

In the future, SMS plans to start short-stay home for needy women with children, undertake documentation and establish research center for Adolescent students, expand the activities of Parisar Vikas in Mumbai and Maharashtra, undertake Awareness campaigns and Water and Waste Management Programme for village women.

The above case[16] illustrates the role of an NGO which is constantly evolving to achieve its mission of reaching to women from all sections of the society by addressing their needs by separate organizational structures to create an impact. This case also highlights that sustainability of an NGO is not a problem as long as they continue to undertake innovative programmes, collaborate with number of organizations and continue to reinvent with the changes in time.

16 ***Source:*** www. karmayog.com, website of Dasra , and inputs received from Pamphlets, in-house articles, www.IndianNGOs.com

Implementation of Government Scheme in Mumbai

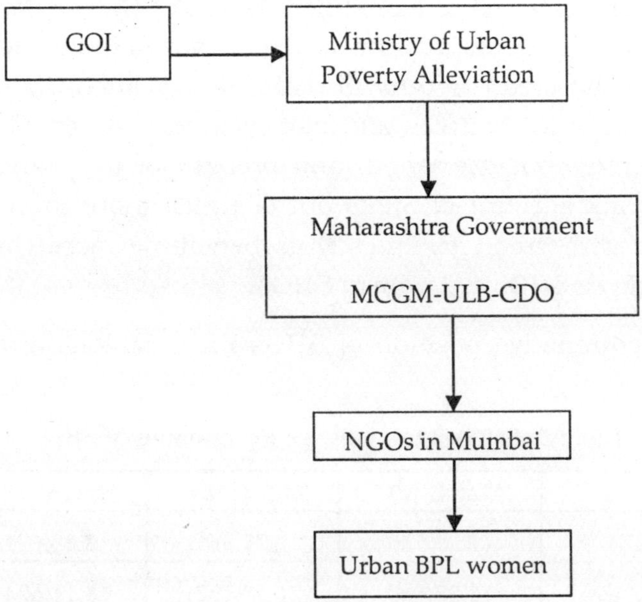

Figure 2: Model of Implementation of SJSRY Scheme

Source: Based on field survey.

Thus, SMS is an example of an NGO which entered into a meaningful dialogue with MCGM to not only provide access of SJSRY scheme to rag pickers but also facilitated the process of micro enterprise development with their innovative initiatives.

- Winning formula **collaboration.**
- Urban Development Department of Government of Maharashtra has noted the importance of this partnership and in its GR of May 2004 has recommended adoption of this approach to all other Municipalities in the state.

Part C — An Assessment of SBI-linked SHGs in the City of Mumbai

SBI is the largest bank in India with over 9,000 branches and is also the largest player in the micro finance sector in India with a market share of around 20%. The bank has been an active participant in the micro finance programmes initiated by NABARD since 1992.

SBI has been actively involved in the micro finance sector as it serves both the social and commercial objectives of the bank. It was the largest player in the micro finance sector in India in terms of loans disbursed to SHGs. It has taken up SHG movement as a mission. A noble mission to reach those families who were hitherto having no access to the credit by any formal financial institution and, therefore, were depending on informal sources and moneylenders. As on March 2006, SBI's branches spread throughout the length and breadth of the country have opened 6,30,067 Savings Bank account of SHGs out of which more than 5.41 lakh SHGs have been provided with credit facilities thus benefiting more than 75 lakh poor people. Majority of these SHGs are women SHGs.

The year-wise cumulative position of SHGs-Bank Linkage Programme for the four years is as under:

Table 9: SHGs-Bank Linkage Programme of SBI

Year	March '03	March '04	March '05	March '06
SHGs linked (financed)	1,07,553	1,74,666	3,43,691	5,40,481
No. of beneficiaries	12,33,660	21,50,752	48,11,674	75,68,842
Amount disbursed	324.84 cr.	614.87 cr.	1311.45 cr.	2262.95 cr.
Amount outstanding	269.43 cr.	462.77 cr.	872.08 cr.	1459.89 cr.
No. of SHGs maintaining Savings a/c in the Bank	2,79,466	3,69,568	5,08,396	6,36,067
Amount in Savings a/c (Amt. in Rs.)	261.36 cr.	348.31 cr.	411.82 cr.	434.07 cr.

SBI – LEADER IN SHG-BANK CREDIT LINKAGE

SBI is maintaining its position as a leader among Commercial Banks in credit linking of SHGs and is a prime driver for the movement. As at the end of March 2006, SBI with a share of approximately 47% of total SHGs financed by Commercial Banks is far ahead of others. Bank has successfully initiated various measures toward widening its SHG network. To list a few examples:

(i) Sensitization of staff: Bank's aim is to sensitize the entire staff from Manager to Messenger working in rural and semi-urban branches towards the programme.

(ii) Special training programmes in SHGs are being conducted at 54 training centres of the bank in the country apart from State Bank Institute of Rural Development, Hyderabad.

(iii) Close liaison with NGOs: Operating functionaries at branch level and region level are in close contact with NGOs in their area to take the movement ahead. For the purpose, regular meetings are arranged with the NGOs and their support is solicited.

(iv) SHG cells: Special SHG cells have been opened at major branches.

(v) Lending to NGOs/Federations of SHGs: Lending to credible NGOs/ Federations of SHGs on selective basis for on lending to SHGs is being encouraged.

(vi) Sahayog Niwas: SBI has launched its Housing Loan product 'SAHAYOG NIWAS' meant for SHG members. Under the scheme formulated keeping the socio-economic conditions of villages insight, housing loans are given to the SHG members without any mortgage of house/land. Response to this product is very encouraging.

(vii) SBI Life-Shakti: SBI Life, our insurance subsidiary, is the first to introduce a life insurance scheme, especially designed for SHG members. Special feature of the scheme is that entire premium amount paid by the member is refunded after maturity, i.e., 10 years.

(viii) Rural training institutes: To help the rural youth to stand on their feet, two RUDSETI type training institutes have been established at Gulbarga and Gadag in Karnataka State, to impart training in self-employment to youth free of cost.

(ix) SBI Staff as Self-help Promoting Institutions: The main role of formation and nurturing of SHGs have been played by NGOs who, apart from their fundamental role of social service, also aim to make the poor economically self-sufficient.

(x) Appreciation by Government: A number of branches/Circles have also received commendation and appreciation from various State Governments for doing excellent job in SHG-Bank Credit Linkage Programme.

(xi) Samanwita: Bank has sponsored and financially supported NGO 'SAMANWITA' in collaboration with Government of Orissa for supplementing the process of socio-economic upliftment of the tribals and the downtrodden in the poorest and most backward Kandhamal district of Orissa State where 52% of the population is that of tribals. Core activities performed by Samanwita are empowerment of people through promotion of SHGs, especially women SHGs and development of human resources.

SBI has adopted two models for financing.

- 30% of the finance is through the first model — SHG-Bank Linkage Model. The model envisages forming small, cohesive and participative groups of the poor, encouraging them to pool their savings regularly and using the pooled thrift for small interest bearing loans to their members and
- The rest of the 70% of finance is through the second model. Under this model, the self-help promoting institution (SHPI), usually a non-governmental organization (NGO), helps groups of 15-20 individuals through an incubation period after which time they are linked to banks. The bank lends to the groups after the incubation period, and this linkage may be single- or multi-period.

Table 10: Comparative Analysis of Delivery Models of Two MFIs in Mumbai City

Particulars	Models	
	SBI	ICICI
Model	Models adopted	Partnership model
Formation of SHGs	SHGs formed by NGOs/MFIs	SHGs formed by MFIs
Finance	SHGs financed through MFIs	SHGs directly financed by banks
Credit Risk	Financial intermediary assumes credit	Bank assumes credit risk
Monitoring Supervision and recovery	MFIs handles the credit monitoring	Banks handles the credit monitoring
Training	Training costs borne by the MFIs	Training costs borne by Banks

Table 11: Profile of SBI Assisted SHG Group

Particulars	Name of the Bachat Ghat		
	Purtata Mahila Swayam Sahayog Bachat Ghat Santacruz (West)	Smruti Triratna Swayam Sahayog Bachat Ghat	Gatee Mahila Swayam Sahayati Bachat Ghat
Location	Santacruz	Santacruz	Santacruz
Managed by	Karuna Kadam-2004	Jyoti Jadhav - 2004	Deepak Vijay Aganwadi
No. of members	13	11	20
Amount sanctioned by SBI	-	86,000/-	-

Amount utilized	-	55,000/-	-
Members contribution	50/-	30/-	50/-
Loan sanctioned to each member	2000/-	2000/-	3000/-
Loan availed by members	13	11	13
Interest charged	-	2%	-

- Prerna Mahila Bachat Ghat Utpatak Ghat in Ghatkopar managed by VIDYA KUSTHALA — award winner.
- SBI has sanctioned a loan of Rs. 2 lakh to the GHAT. The contributions of all the SHG groups are deposited in SBI.
- The Ghat provides training to both the groups for the production. The groups are:
  - **(1) EKTA SAMAJVIKAS SAMASTHA:** EKTA has 18 SHGs, and the members in each group is 10. They produce candles, agarbattis, phenyl, perfumes, shampoo, detergent powder, liquid soap, etc. There are 18 SHGs under it.
  - **(2) SWATI SAMAJVIKAS SAMSTHA:** SWATI has 13 groups and the members in each group is 10. They make bags and provide food to BMC school students. There are 13 groups under it.
- **The SHGs in Shell Colony and Tilak Nagar Chembur:** The groups are not into any activity since they not received any training. But they collect the members' contributions and they avail the loans for their personal requirements. There are 20 members in each group. In some groups, they contribute Rs. 50/- per head and the other groups contribute Rs. 100 per member. Each member has availed loans upto Rs. 25,000/- for their personal requirements from SBI. The contributions of the SHGs are deposited in SBI.

Thus, from the above analysis, we can make out that SBI-linked SHG have had a domino effect on the formation of other SHGs in the nearby vicinity.

- According to the Centre head, Vidya Khustale, the reach of the SHG in Ghatkopar is around 4000 women.
- This proves the fact that with little support from MFIs, the women can be empowered to move out of the circle of poverty and take care of their personal lives.

Analysis of Findings of Survey of SBI-linked SHGs in City of Mumbai

1. Profile of the respondent: This variable was used to examine the age group to which the micro entrepreneurs belong. Out of the 24 women surveyed, 67% members were in the age group of 25-45.

***2. Educational qualification*:** This variable was used to assess the educational level of respondents, in order to find out the educational qualification of respondents. It was found out that 70.83% women were educated below 9th standard and 20.83% women were illiterate. This figure illustrates the fact that these women have no choice but to approach the NGOs for vocational training as the minimum qualification required to join Regional Vocational Training Institute (RVTI) is 10th standard.

3. Earlier occupation of those who migrated (multiple response): This variable is used to assess how many amongst them had an experience of micro enterprise development prior to migrating to Mumbai. It has been observed that the women played multiple roles. Out of the 24 women, 25% were self-employed, 45.83% were wage earners and 25% were housewives.

4. Establishment of micro enterprise and reason(s) for change to micro enterprise development: This variable has been included to verify the stage at which the micro enterprise was established by the married women and reasons for starting the micro enterprise by women surveyed in general. Out of the 47 married women, 38 started the enterprise post marriage and 9 started the enterprise before marriage.

5. Reason for change to self-employment: This variable was analyzed to assess the switch over to self-employment. It was observed that 50% women started micro enterprise with the possibility of improving income, 37.5% started the micro enterprise because of low earning in previous activity and because of health problems which stopped them from traveling long distance for work and migration of family.

6. Motivation to join SHG: This variable was used to evaluate whether women join the SHG group out of compulsion or whether they were influenced by some members from their social group. It was observed that group leaders played an important role in influencing members to join the SHG 83.33% women were influenced them. In the SHGs covered in our study, we realized that Ms. Vidya Khustale of Ghatkopar has played a major role in influencing the SHG members. Apart from this, 16.67% women said that they were influenced by friends.

7. Level of income: The level of women's empowerment depends to a great extent on a women's ability to earn an income and support the family. Depending upon the group to which the member belonged and the number of years involved with the SHG, the approximate monthly salary varied to a great extent. It was noticed that the group leaders were not only involved in the SHGs but also had their own independent business enterprise and the family also was very supportive of their activities. The members of Purthata SHG which has completed 7 years, the average monthly income ranged from 2000 to 4500, as these women were very enterprising and have started 11 business activities simultaneously. This proves that in order to earn a substantial income it is necessary to provide multiple skills training to these women as then the members can decide amongst themselves the products they would be dealing in and the market are they would cover individually.

8. Nature of assistance received from the above organization: As the respondents were linked with the NGO for their livelihood, the researcher wanted to assess the support provided to these micro entrepreneurs. 66.67% members received assistance for loan and maximum members stated that they received moral support.

9. Loans availed: This variable was used to assess the level of indebtedness amongst the micro entrepreneurs. It has been observed that only 66.67% availed the loan. Some respondents have taken multiple loans. 41.7% MERs availed of loan to meet emergency expenses, 25% respondents availed of the loan for consumption purpose and only 20.83% availed loan for income generation activities.

10. Sources of availing loan: This variable was used to assess whether the micro entrepreneurs still depended on moneylenders for their requirements. 50% women availed loans from SHGs and it was surprising to note that they did not approach moneylenders and few approached banks for loans.

11. Nature of business activity: This variable is used to verify the trading activities of the micro entrepreneurs. 12.5% of the micro entrepreneurs were engaged in tailoring. On further enquiry as to the legal status of their enterprise, 37.5% micro entrepreneurs stated that it was a sole enterprise, 83.33% MERs worked under a registered partnership firm.

12. Constraints faced by the MER in the process of micro enterprise development: At the entry level, lack of skill was cited by 29.7% as a major drawback. Followed by 20.83% entrepreneurs who remarked that there was inadequate information about availability of raw material at cheap price.

Problems encountered by the NGOs

- NGOs stated that the major constraints faced by the NGOs were lack of motivated beneficiaries and irregular attendance.
- NGOs stated that they were unable to find loyal customers for the products on a regular basis.

Recommendations

- Government should take a review of the best practices of grassroots organizations and provide wide publicity to their efforts and provide them with necessary assistance without procedural delays.
- The corporate can have a meaningful dialogue with NGOs and organize NGO Melas in their premises.
- Government through its extensive network should ensure adequate support for the beneficiaries to enable them to market their products.
- Institutions like Central leather institute can play a proactive role by training women to manufacture and market leather products.
- Participatory approach to Development is the need of the hour. Academic institutions can and should partner with the third sector to impart training to SHG women. For example: As a part of the outreach programme SIES College of Commerce and Economics (Mumbai) organized a social enterprise training programme titled **"Train the Trainer".** This programme aimed at empowering women by providing micro enterprise training to members of Self-help Groups in order to enable them to act as a catalyst for change. In all, 27 women from 7 Bachat Ghats from Santacruz, Kanjurmarg and Dharavi participated in this event. The training programme was imparted by Ms. Vidya Kustale and Ms. Manju, members of SHG from Purthathata Mahila Bachat Ghat from Ghatkopar.

Conclusion

This study showed that NGOs play an important role of empowering women through provision of micro finance and micro enterprise development programmes. The poor women needed training to develop skills and self-confidence to allow them to operate and survive in the informal sector. Access to credit is important but not sufficient for the poorest women. Therefore the role of NGOs, in imparting training for enterprise development is a right step in enabling empowerment of poor women. Micro enterprises have been identified as high potential sector for employee's generation and source of livelihood to millions of people in Asian, African and Latin American countries. Thus, entrepreneurship development training among urban poor beneficiaries could prove to be one of the most effective strategies for urban poverty alleviation through creation of self and wage employment opportunities by provision of appropriate Business development services along with provision of micro finance.

Bibliography

1. ICFAI, January, 2007, Micro Finance: A Promoting Instrument for SHGs.
2. Thomas Fisher and M.S. Sriram, Beyond Micro Credit.
3. Dasgupta Rajaram, 2005, Micro Finance in India — Empirical Evidence, Alternative Models and Policy Imperatives, *Economic and Political Weekly*, 19th March, 07.
4. http://www.iimahd.ernet.in/~mssriram/microfinance-RT.pdf
5. http://www.rbh.in/Home/pdf/Micro_Finance_by_ICICI.pdf
6. http://www4.gsb.columbia.edu/null/download?&exclusive=filemgr.download&file_id=646440
7. http://www.ipfindia.org/pdfs/icici_studies.pdf
8. www.cgap.org/commercialbanks/profiles.html

Appendix

1. List of NGOs surveyed in Mumbai.

ACT	ACT-Kalpana
AMM	Annapurna Mahila Mandal
APN	Apnalaya
BECC	Bandra East Community Centre
CASP	Community Aid and Sponsorship Programme
CORP	Community Out Reach Programme
CH	Creative Handicrafts
FSC	Family Service Centre
GVPCT	Gyan Vikas Public Charitable Trust
JCT	Janvi Charitable Trust
REAP	Reach Education Action Programme
SHARE	Save the Handicapped's Rehabilitation Efforts
SMS	Stree Mukti Sanghatana
SF	Sterlite Foundation
USVA	Urban Street Lok Seva Kendra
VT	Vatsalya Trust
YUVA	Youth for Unity and Voluntary Action
YUVAK	Yuvak Prathishtan
SHED	Support for Human and Environmental Development

3

Micro Finance Plus Services — Need of the Day

Shri Hemanth Kumar,
Group Vice President, Basix

The Context

The Poor in India Faced

- Unfulfilled livelihood needs
- Low access to markets, information and financial services
- Unmanaged risks
- Geographical and social exclusion
- Low productivity
- Low price realization

Opportunity Knocks

"War on nations changes maps. War on poverty maps change."

— ***Muhammad Ali***

Waging the war to make a difference:

- Fighting the unfavorable policy and regulatory framework
- Fulfilling unfulfilled needs – financial access, risk mitigation, skill enhancement, Business Development Services
- Bridging the gap between the needs and access to the entire gamut of livelihood promotion services

Challenges and Scope

- SKS entered – IPO
- RBI internal panel recommend — NBFC loans are not Priority sector.
- Money will talk on mobile phones
- 125 NBFC-MFIs
- Translating NGO to MFI
- Multiple financing – competition
- Scope for livelihood intervention

MICRO FINANCE

Micro finance is a set of financial services extended to socially and economically disadvantaged segments of society.

(a) Savings

(b) Credit

(c) Insurance

(d) Other Support Services known as CREDIT PLUS

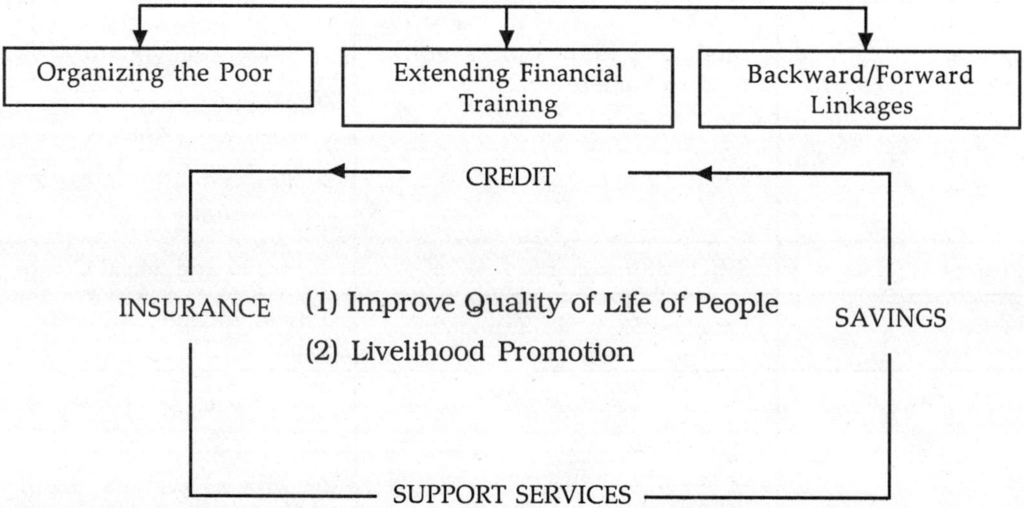

Why Micro Finance?

1. To improve the quality of the people
2. To reduce the dependency culture
3. To reduce exploitation
4. To meet the financial requirements of the poor and downtrodden including women

Breaking the Vicious Cycle of Poverty

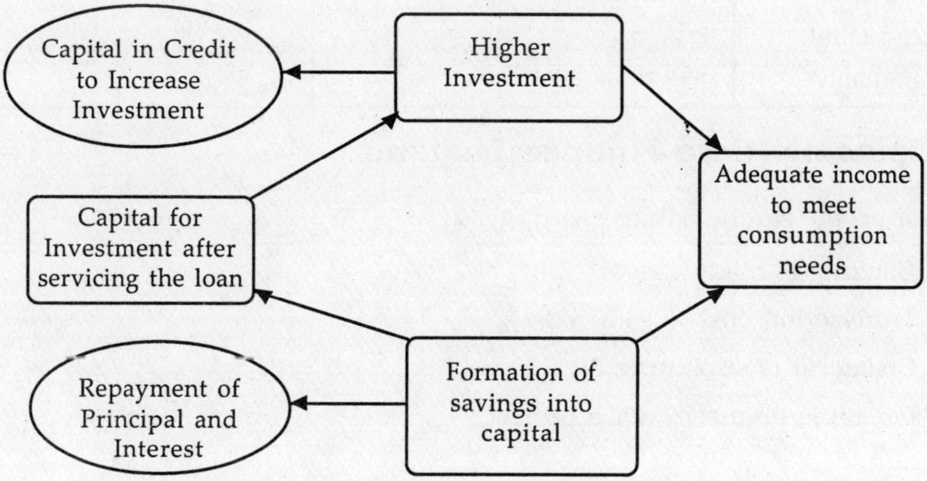

Commercial Banking vs. Micro Finance

	Commercial Banking	Micro Finance
Mission	Provide financial services products with favorable returns to shareholders	❖ Provide financial services to a low income group ❖ Higher access to poor including women ❖ Favorable returns to shareholder
Services	Strictly Financial	Financial and Social Components
Clientele	Large Scale, Well off, Literate	Lower income, Illiterate, Small Scale
Administration/Loan Process	Complex/Loan delivery is not prompt	Simple (Prompt loan delivery)
Savings	Does not mobilise small savings (Rural Areas)	Mobilise Savings from low income
Collateral Requirements	Property can be mortgaged	No Collateral up to certain limit < 50k
Repayment Rate	Recovery Rate are lower	Very high repayment rates
Customer Support	Little or No Support to clients	❖ Strong Service Provider Relationship ❖ Monitoring Mechanism ❖ Other Support Services
Costs (a) Financial (b) Accessibility (c) Opportunity	 Lower Complex Not Prompt	 Higher Simple Prompt

Principles of Micro Finance Lending

Poor people can be banked with, if:

- ❖ Banking is made easy
- ❖ Transaction cost is reduced
- ❖ Collateral is substituted
- ❖ Person is financed, not a project

- ❖ Peers are involved
- ❖ Borrower pays small sum, frequently

Methods of Micro Finance

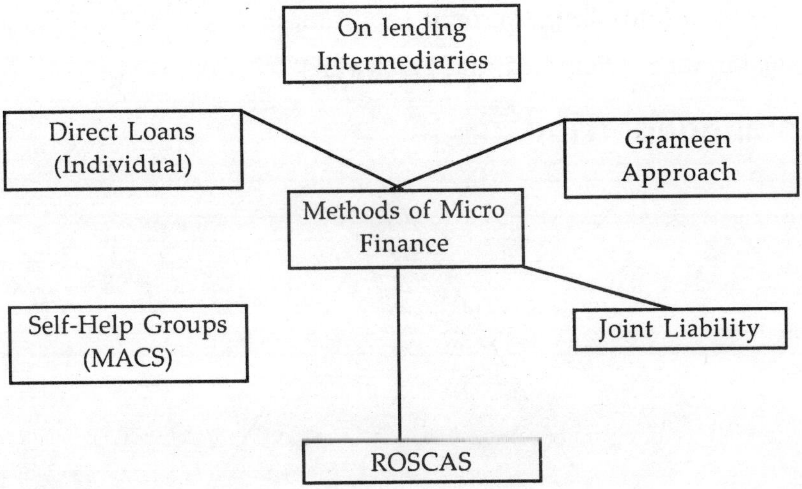

Evolution of Strategy

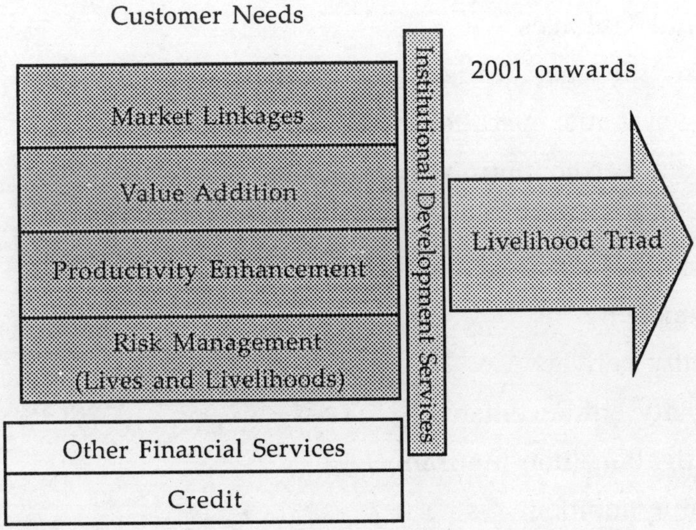

TASS

- IBEX – Inter Borrower exchange
- ERAP – External Resource Advisory Programme
- RIR – Rural Infrastructure Revive
- SHG QIP – Quality Improvement Programme
- Market Linkage – Forward and Backward

BASIX Livelihood Triad

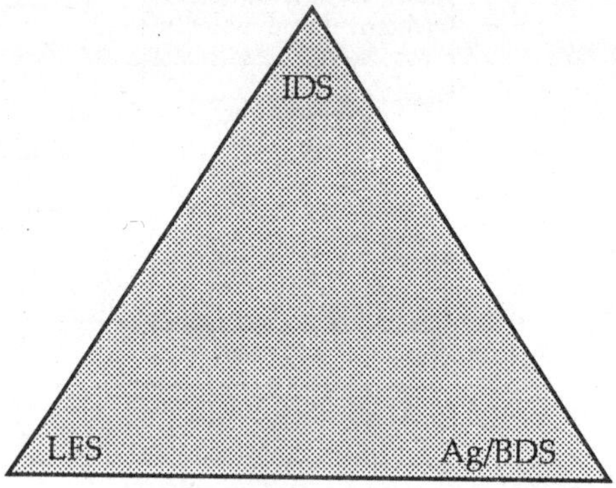

- Organize
- Functional Linkages
- Formalize: the legal status
- Enabling systems: operations, HR and MIS-IT
- Revive: defunct community organizations
- Savings, Credit (short-term as well as long-term)
- Insurance, for lives and livelihoods
- Fund transfers
- Commodity derivatives
- Productivity enhancement
- Risk mitigation (non-insurance)
- Local value addition
- Alternate Market Linkages — Input supply, output sales

Collaborative Polygon

We believe in collaborating with players having domain expertise to................

Enhance competencies, Increase outreach, Reduce transaction costs and Reduce risk for BASIX and its customers

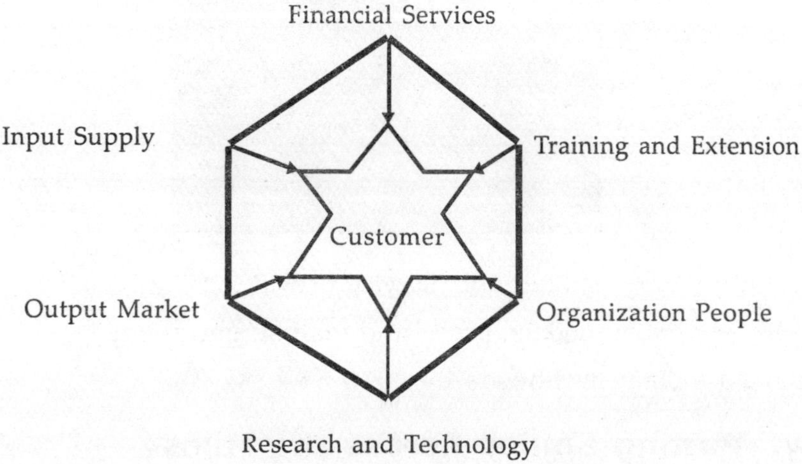

Think Globally Act Locally Do Cooperatively Start Immediately

INSPIRATION FROM LORD GANEṆESHJEE

Lord Ganeshjee's **BIG HEAD** inspires us to think big and think profitably; the **BIG EARS** prompt us to listen patiently to new ideas and suggestions; the **NARRO EYES** point to deep concentration needed to finish tasks in hand well and quickly; the **LONG NOSE** tell us to poke around inquisitively to learn more and the **SMALL MOUTH** reminds us to speak less and listen more.

The Crusade Continues.....to

- Be an innovative, sustainable service provider
- Develop workable models, prove and mainstream them
- Reach 10 million livelihoods by 2015

Basically.. Putting Smiles Across the Miles

THANK YOU

■■■

4

Hindhustan Micro Finance Private Limited

Mr. Chetnanda Rao,
Group Vice President, Hindhustan Micro Finance Pvt. Ltd.,

HINDHUSTAN MICRO FINANCE PRIVATE LIMITED

Hindhustan Bhavan
Ambedkar Nagar, Kurla Andheri Raod,
Kurla (W). Mumbai - 400 072
India

Contact:
Mr. Anil Jadhav
Chairman and Managing Director
E-mail: aniljadhav@hindhustanmfi.com
Mobile: + 91 9 22 23 6 22 44

Contents

About Us

Background

(a) Hindhustan Cooperative Society: Background

- Hindhustan Cooperative started its operations in 1987.
- Led by Anil Jadhav who has 20+ years in urban micro finance.
- Overall the senior management of Hindhustan Cooperative has experience of more than 60 years.
- Primarily target clientele — lower and lower middle class population of suburban Mumbai and Thane.
- Current outreach - 9 branches, 14,500 members.

(b) NBFC Started to offer Micro Finance Services in a Professional Manner

- Hindhustan Micro Finance Pvt. Ltd. (HMPL), an NBFC has been started to offer micro finance services in a more efficient and effective manner and to achieve scale.
- Mr. Anil Jadhav, an experienced Cooperator based in Mumbai and Mr. L.B. Prakash who has 20 years of experience each come together along with other well-wishers.
- NBFC promotes individual and group-based credit products for consumption and business needs, with different repayment frequencies to suit the cash flows of clients — weekly and monthly.
- The size of loan products varies from Rs. 5,000 to Rs. 50,000.

Vision

"To Create a Global Economy of Abundance by Promoting Financial & Technical Inclusion"

To create a global economy of abundance: HMPL is committed to work with poor in the urban areas, especially Mumbai. HMPL wants to develop sustainable micro finance operations in urban areas which could be replicated internationally for the benefit of the poor people.

By promoting financial and technical inclusion: Along with financing, HMPL also plans to provide guidance to its clients about the most profitable use of the money so that the clients benefit the maximum and do not face any problem in repaying the money back in time.

Mission

"To provide appropriate financial services to 2,00,000 poor clients by 2015, in order to help them improve financial management and risk mitigation and develop a replicable urban micro finance model"

Appropriate financial services: HMPL will provide adequate financing to its clients based on their cash flows and requirements so that they do not fall in the debt trap and use the finance for their development.

200,000 clients by 2015: HMPL wants to reach out to a total of 200,000 clients by 2015 through its different loan products.

Improved financial management and risk mitigation: Through its cash flow based financial services HMPL wants to improve the condition of its clients so that they are able to manage their finances in the most productive manner and reduce the risk in their lives.

Develop a replicable urban micro finance model: Micro finance in urban settings is a relatively new phenomenon in India. Again the urban scenario in Mumbai is more complex than other urban settings in India. Therefore, HMPL wants to develop a micro finance model which is not only successful in Mumbai but also replicable in urban settings like Mumbai.

Mumbai Market Opportunity

(a) Size of potential credit demand

Population c. 18m with c. 54% living in slums[1] and c. 75% living in poverty. The estimated demand for credit in Mumbai is c. Rs. 2,400 crores ($480m)[2] based just on the proportion of population living in slums.

---

1. Census of India 2001
2. 18m × 54% living in slums/average 5 members per household × annual demand of $242 (average loan size for top 50 global MFIs as per DB 2007 Microfinance report)

(b) Customer Profile – Slums/Autorickshaw Market

Men and women of 20-50 years who are in the category of lower (poor) and lower middle class section of population, with monthly earnings varying from Rs. 3,500 to Rs. 10,000.

Mainly daily bread earners with activities like domestic help, vegetable selling, manufacturing and construction labour, autorickshaw drivers, etc.

Typically borrow for regular needs (purchase of stock, investment in business, education, repayment of moneylender loans, marriage, etc.) and sudden needs (medical, work loss, etc.) to capital needs (purchase of autorickshaw, starting new business, etc.)[3]

(c) Competition[4]

Large Co-operative Societies and Co-operative Banks – estimated number: 30-50; total outreach: 500,000 to 1 million

Banks and large NBFCs, estimated number: 5-10; Estimated total outreach: 20,000-50,000

MFIs: Estimated number: 4-5

SWOT Analysis

Strengths	Weaknesses
❖ Committed leadership. ❖ Two decades of experience in urban micro finance. ❖ Young and trained management team, with good understanding of the market and its dynamics.	❖ New entrant in formal micro finance — the systems and staff need to be tuned for micro finance (e.g., reporting and monitoring of PAR, reporting of arrears, training for audit and monitoring, etc.) ❖ Experience in Mumbai only.
Opportunities	**Threats**
❖ Large, unserved market in Mumbai and other towns in Maharashtra. ❖ Potential to become a national-level urban MFI.	❖ Possible competition from stronger NBFCs.

3 & 4 HMPL research

Clientele and Loan Product

Parameters	JLG Loan	Individual Loan
Clientele Profile	Women entrepreneurs organized into groups of 5 clients	Women or men
Purpose	Working capital, investment or consumption needs	Working capital, investment or consumption needs
Loan Amount	Rs. 5,000-Rs. 25,000	Rs. 25,000-Rs. 50,000
Loan Term	50 weeks	6-18 months
Repayment Frequency	Weekly	Monthly
Collateral Security	Group guarantee + 8% Advanced EWI (upfront)	Post-dated cheques, Property documents (in some cases) + 8% Advanced EMI upfront
Interest rate/yield	15% Flat	15% Flat

Progress as on August 31, 2010

Sr. No.	Loan Product	Clients	Loan Outstanding (Rs.)
1.	Individual Loan (PDC)	65	8,66,763
2.	JLG	7,266	4,09,17,922

Supported through 9 Branches and 71 Staff.

Progress as on August 31, 2010

- **Systems and Processes**
  - Developed robust Operational Processes for its Loan Products, particularly JLG.
  - Operational Processes for the Individual (PDC) loan received the RBS MPEA Award in the Flint category (start-ups), for the Western Region.

❖ **Support from Financial Institutions**

— Yes Bank, Axis Bank, HDFC, DCB, SBI

❖ **MIS Development**

— MIS is developed currently, with the Accounting option being integrated with Portfolio.

❖ **Internal Control**

— Developed internal team for management audit and appointed independent auditor of internal audit.

PlaNet Finance

RBS

This is to certify that

Hindusthan Microfinance Private Limited

has been adjudged

Regional Winner, West

in the Flint category of the

Microfinance Process Excellence Awards 2008

MPEA Award: November 24, 2008

Governance (as of August 31, 2010)

Sl. No.	Name/Designation	Brief Profile
1.	Anil Jadhav Chairman and Managing Director.	20+ years' experience in Cooperatives and Urban Micro Finance. Promoter and Chairman of Hindhustan Cooperative Proprietor of Hindhustan IT Solutions Ltd., which supplies MIS software to Co-operative Societies in Maharashtra.
2.	L.B. Prakash Director	Management graduate with c 20 years' experience in micro finance. Consulted for various Indian and International agencies including the UN, CGAP, MISFA, CARE, Grameen Foundation, EDA/M-CRIL and MicroSave.

We are in the process of expanding out BOD through individual as well as institutional participation.

Management Team

Sl. No.	Name/Designation	Brief Profile
1.	Anil Jadhav Chairman and Managing Director	20+ years' experience in Urban Micro Finance and Cooperative management. Promoter and Chairman of Hindhustan Cooperative. Proprietor of Hindhustan IT Solutions Ltd., which supplies MIS software to cooperative societies in Maharashtra.
2.	L.B. Prakash Director and Consultant	Management graduate with 16+ years' experience in micro finance. Has consulted for various Indian and international agencies including the UN, CARE, Grameen Foundation, EDA/M-CRIL and MicroSave.
3.	Chetananand M. Raut V.P.- Operation	Engineering and MBA graduate having more than 13 years of experience. Areas of expertise include strategic business planning and execution, change management, human resource management, MIS development, institutional development and governance, project management and finance.
4.	Dheeraj Sudanshu Regional Coordinator	3+ years' experience in micro finance operations with BASIX and VWS – two well-known MFIs in India.

Brief Profile of Anil Jadhav

Anil Jadhav is the founder of Hindhustan IT Solutions (HITS), a software company which has developed handheld devices and accounting software in Cooperative Credit Societies. The accounting software is being used at Hindhustan Cooperative and over 500 Cooperative Credit Societies in Maharashtra. He is also currently:

- *Chairman* of the *Hindhustan Cooperative Credit Society (HCCS).*
- *Secretary* of the *Mumbai Purva Upanagari Sahakari Padasansthanche* Federation Ltd. (Mumbai North East District Cooperative Credit Societies Federation – MNE DCCS Fed.), which has over 600 Cooperative Credit Societies as its members.
- Director of the Sarvodaya Cooperative Bank Ltd., Mumbai.
- Founder-Director of the Khatau Taluka Cooperative Credit Society Ltd.
- Chairman of the Khatau Taluka Rehwasi Sanghatana.
- Founder-Chairman of Hindhustan Micro Finance Private Limited.
- Formerly Director of the Maharashtra State Coopèrative Credit Societies Federation.

Our Clients – Some Case Studies

CASE STUDY - 1

Name	:	Mr. U.P. Udayshankar
Age	:	40 years
Occupation	:	Tailoring Shop
Loan Product	:	Ezee Loan
Amount	:	Rs. 5,000 ($100)
Repayment Terms	:	Rs. 50 per day for 100 days

- ❖ Uday is from Belgaum district of Bordering Karnataka and for last 20 years he is staying in Kurla (W) of Mumbai. He has family of three – wife and a son who studies in school.
- ❖ He has a tailoring shop where he employs two more tailors based on need and pays them on a per piece basis. His monthly earning is Rs. 10,000 and saves about Rs. 3,000 per month.
- ❖ He has taken loan of Rs. 5,000 from HMPL as an "Ezee Loan" for his family needs which he repays as Rs. 50 daily for 100 days.
- ❖ Uday, happy with HMPL, want to take a larger loan to purchase stock and increase his business.

CASE STUDY - 2

Name	:	Baban Shinde
Age	:	50 years
Occupation	:	Cobbler
Loan Product	:	Individual Loan
Amount	:	Rs. 40,000 ($800)
Repayment Terms	:	18 months

- ❖ Baban is from rural Maharashtra and has a small Footwear Shop near Saki-Naki Junction, Mumbai, where he makes all the traditional leather footwear — which is still in good demand.
- ❖ During the peak season, he has a monthly earning of Rs. 12,500. During the monsoon, his sale goes down and soon after he requires a substantial amount to purchase raw material (leather) as demand steeps up again. After all family expenses and loan repayments, he has a net saving of about Rs. 3,000 which he saves in Banks and co-operative credit societies.
- ❖ Baban has taken an Individual Loan of Rs. 40,000 from HMPL to purchase leather stock.
- ❖ Baban is now dreaming big and would like a bigger loan of Rs. 1,00,000 to put-up a bigger shop.

CASE STUDY - 3

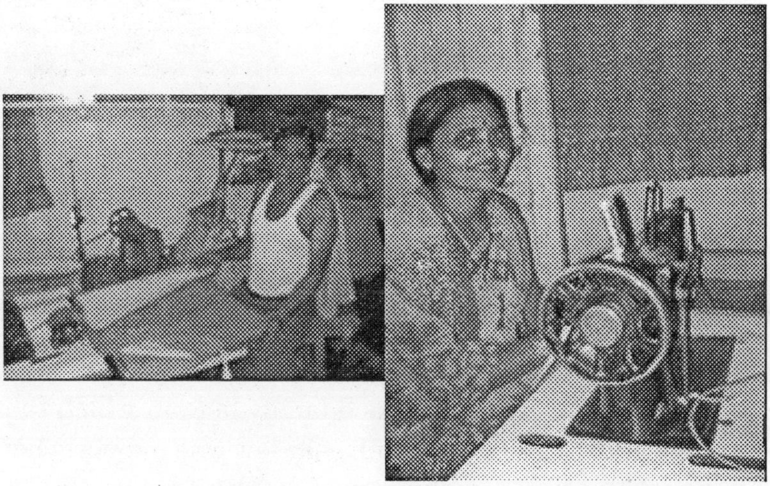

Name	:	Lalita
Age	:	36 years
Occupation	:	Tailor
Loan Product	:	Joint Liability Group
Amount	:	Rs. 5,000 ($100)
Repayment Terms	:	Rs. 240 per week

- Lalita is from Latur District, Maharashtra, she along with her husband, Namdev shifted to Mumbai in 1985 as there was no job back home.
- Lalita and Namdev do tailoring for their livelihood and have a total monthly earning of Rs. 12,000.
- She took the loan of Rs. 5,000 to purchase a sewing machine which has increased their productivity and now she could save up to Rs. 2,000 per month.
- Lalita, happy with the JLG Loan experience and the benefit of having a sewing machine now wants to take a larger loan of Rs. 50,000 for renting a space and purchasing more sewing machines.

CASE STUDY - 4

Name	:	Shaila Patel
Age	:	40 years
Occupation	:	Electric Switch Assembler
Loan Product	:	Joint Liability Group
Amount	:	Rs. 5,000 ($100)
Repayment Terms	:	Rs. 50 per day for 100days

- Shaila, is from Beed district, Maharashtra, and staying in Mumbai with her family for the past 25 years. She has a family of 8, in which there are 3 more earners — husband, a driver; her brother-in-law who supports her in the Switch Assembling and her son, a technician.
- Shaila has a monthly savings of Rs. 4,000 and is also maintaining a Saving Account with Hindusthan Co-operative Credit Society for last several years.
- Shaila took the loan from HMPL to repay the loan taken by mortgaging her jewellery and also for festival celebrations.
- She is repaying her loan regularly and at a later date wants to take a bigger loan from HMPL to purchase an autorickshaw for her son.

Our Partners in Progress

HDFC BANK

YES BANK
EXPERIENCE OUR EXPERTISE

RBS
The Royal Bank of Scotland Group

AXIS BANK

MicroSave
Market-led solutions for financial services

DCB

भारतीय स्टेट बैंक
State Bank of India
With you - all the way

FWWB

Our Future Plans

Present and Proposed Branch Spread

FY 2009	FY 2010	FY 2011
Jarimari, Antop Hill	Kalva, Mankhurd, Dharavi, Bhandup, Vikroli	Expansion in smaller towns in Maharashtra like Solapur, Nagar, etc.
	Pune: Kothrud, Dattawadi, Yerwada, Bhosari	

Business Plan Summary

Portfolio Data	Mar-10	Mar-11	Mar-12	Mar-13	Mar-14	Mar-15
Number of Branches	6	7	15	30	45	65
Portfolio Outstanding (Cr.)	3.40	6.82	16.14	43.04	88.72	149.82
Total Number ofEemployees	50	120	239	406	718	1135
Number of Active Loans	5,649	13,623	30,108	60,094	120,093	200,094

Present Organogram

Hindhustan Micro Finance Pvt. Ltd., Organogram: June 17, 2010

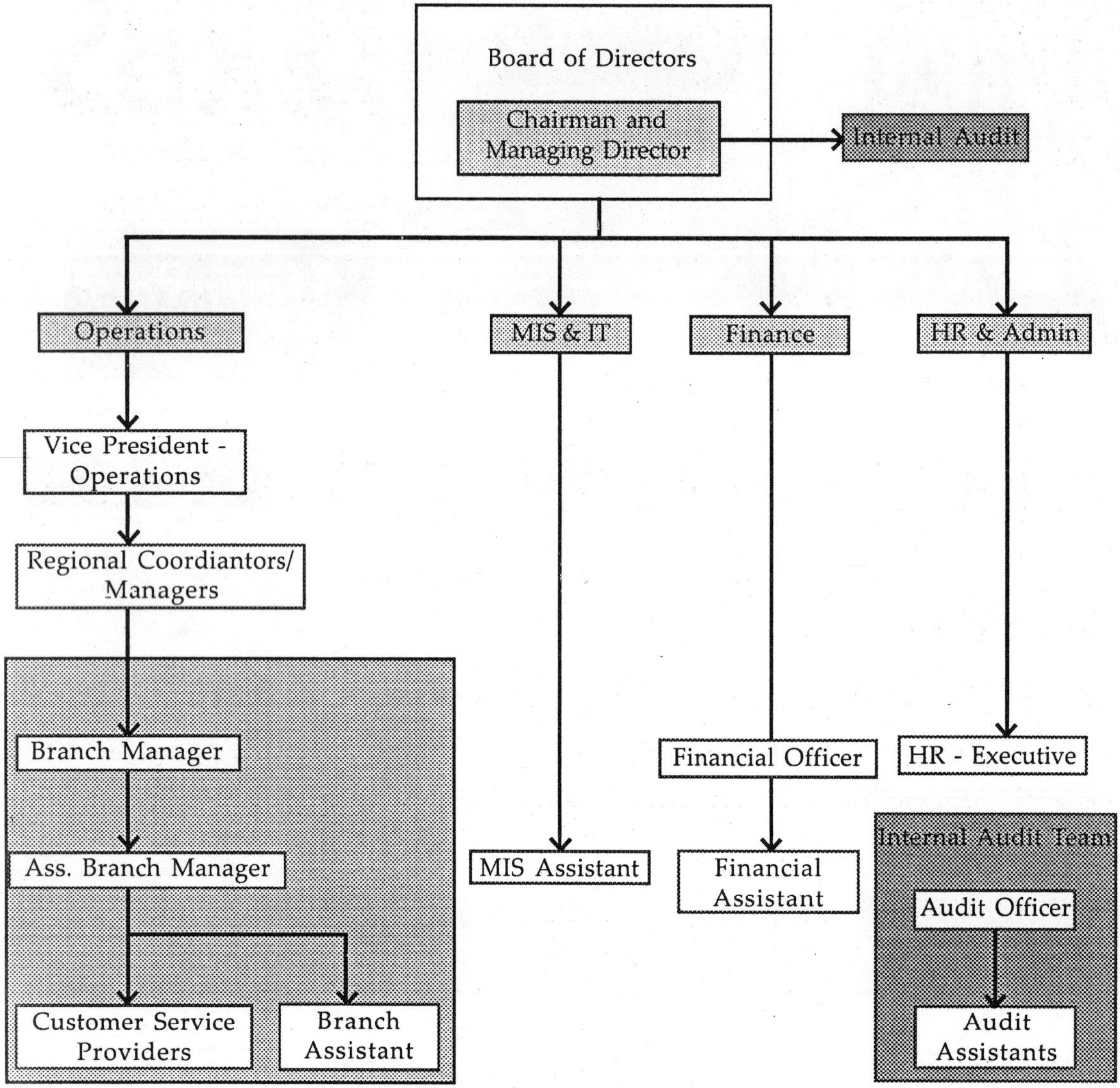

Proposed Organogram

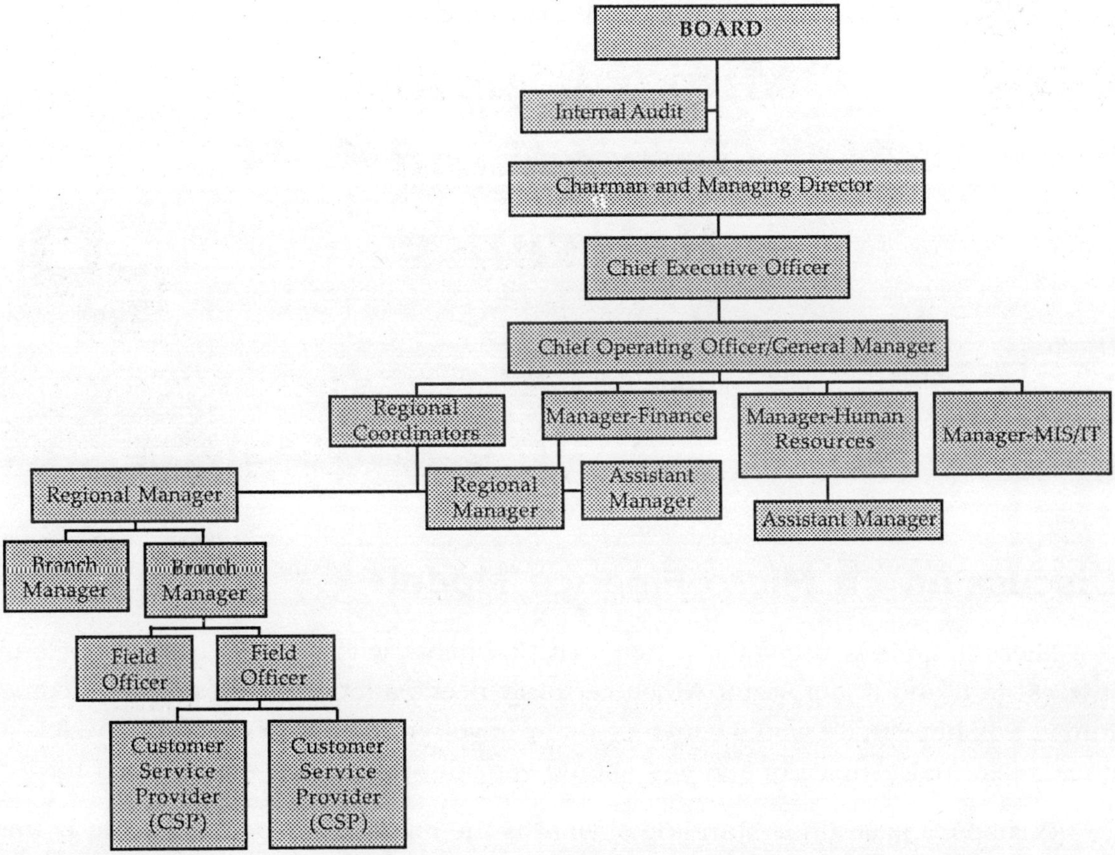

Thank You.

■■■

5

Micro Finance: Issues and Relevance

Mrs. Radhika HariBhakti, Director,
Spandan Micro Finance Ltd.

Discussion on Micro Finance Model*

Micro finance is becoming a topic with students who want to hear about our interest in it and it is a sector which certainly needs a lot of young people to come into it. So I hope that I would convince many of you at the end of my talk. There is a great sector to be a part of and you should consider joining the sector, like I have.

Perhaps, a good understanding of what is the micro finance model, what is the government promoting? NABARD promoted SHG and bank linkage model and the basic aspects of how micro finance work is needed.

Typically that there is no collateral, that is a weekly repayment. Is this micro finance sector going the same route as the subprime mortgage sector, which really has been responsible for this huge mess in the financial system around the world, because it started in the US and then it has kind of snowballed into all economies? India has not been hit much by it, thankfully. So I am going to address whether this concern is at all valid, and since I believe it is not, I am going to of course substantiate it with the basic differences between what happened in the subprime mortgage problem, and what micro finance sector is all about and therefore cannot have the kind of problems that we saw there. Perhaps, these comments and observations that have appeared stem from either lack of clear understanding of the micro finance sector, or clear understanding of the subprime mortgage problem, or maybe both.

*(Text of the speech delivered by Mrs.Radhika Haribhakti, Director, Spandan Spoorthy Financials Limted)

So to start with, I first very briefly describe what the subprime problem was. The subprime mortgage problem in US has typically happened because, number one, very low interest rates in the US, a whole approach of lenders to push their product to the borrowers, regardless of their capacity to repay, and this problem was compounded by the fact that there were all these fancy structured products, that derivative products, which in fact transferred the credit risk of those mortgages, to not the initial lender of the loan, but some other investor who may not even be in that country. It can be anywhere in the world.

So what had happened was, that supposes in California, a local bank like Bank of America may have given loans to borrowers there, they think they unpackaged that credit risk and say, sold it to an investor in Hong Kong. The investor in Hong Kong thought that this was giving excellent yield on the investment, so they in turn leverage themselves, which means if they had $100 million to invest, they would borrow another $400 million, $500 million and then invest as much as $500 million, $600 million on a mortgage portfolio. And to start with the problem was that most of these borrowers, they borrowed this kind of loan at such a low interest rate of 2 or 3%, that somebody who is financially-savvy would think that this is the kind of rent that I would anyway pay on a house like this, so why not I buy, pay an installment, an EMI, which is very much on the lines of what you would pay for a rental, and therefore they would take that regardless of their ability to pay.

Another thing which we had to take into account is that most of these borrowers were parked on the mainstream economy of the US. It was not like going to the financially excluded sections, if there is any such section in the US. So when the whole economy started slowing down, two things happened. A lot of these borrowers lost their jobs, and therefore they overnight lost the ability to repay. Also the interest rates went up, and as many of you would appreciate, the consumerism in US is so high that people have hardly any savings. So if interest rates and your EMI goes up by just even 5%, there is no backup of savings to fall back on.

In India generally, most people would be trying to save, even the low income households like to put away some money as a saving, which is not what happens there. So as a result, too many defaults happened, and the defaults did not just hit the immediate lender in the US, but investors around the world, who suddenly found that they had lent on the assumption of the value of the collateral, which is those houses, and now that their value had collapsed. So this is just to describe what happened there.

What is micro finance lending all about? See, in India, micro finance started and we were just hearing someone who talked about the NGO movement, it really started as a not-for-profit NGO movement, with the intention of helping women from very low income group, with small loans which would get them started with some small business. To given an example, an Rs. 5,000 loan can help a woman in a village, for example, set up a small tea stall for example. As she cannot set it up on her own, because she does not have the means to buy the typical vessels, or the cups in which she would serve and sell them tea, or even the tea, the working capital, it's just not there. They don't have the means to even start a small business like that. Micro finance gives that money; she is able to set it up, the cash flows of such businesses, small businesses micro businesses are really very robust. She is able to repay the loans, and then the way the growth of these small businesses happen is from selling just tea, she did, maybe in the second year loan, invest something in a few glasses, jars, in which she will buy and put some biscuits and sweets and other things. So the same clients who come to her, to buy a cup of tea, may also buy these other things. That's the kind of growth that happens through micro finance. The kind of dreams the borrowers of micro finance have would be that he could start as a vegetable vendor, starting with a small basket of vegetables she carries from door to door to sell, her next dream would be to have a cart, in which she can carry more vegetables, move around more easily, and sell more, and from there the dream would take her on to the next level of growth, which would be a shop. So these are the kind of businesses that micro finance supports, because all financing of productive income generating activities, there are comments people make and how do you monitor that?

Well, some of it could be used for personal consumption, ultimately money is fungible, you can't really — that happens with corporate also, so there is nothing unique, but ultimately it enhances the income of income families. And what started as an NGO movement, grew but in a very limited way, because it was constantly dependent on availability of grant money. So some amounts of profits maybe there, but ultimately grant was required for these NGOs to grow, and as you can appreciate, no model of any activity or business can be sustainable, with just the support of grant. So few years back, quite a few commercial providers of capital, recognized this as a very robust, viable business model, also highly scalable and they came in and brought in a lot of capital. So, the not-for-profit sector eventually converted into a for-profit sector and after the capital came in, there has been a tremendous growth in the sector. The small NGOs that started years ago, have now become extremely large financial institutions, to just give you some kind of a sense for the numbers, between the top say 7 to 10 micro finance institutions, the outreach would be as much as 18 to 20 million borrowers.

So that is the kind of outreach, and we can talk of course about the portfolio sized, but to my mind the most interesting thing that micro finance does is reaching out to so many people. Let us accept that the banking sector, the formal banking sector could never have reached out to these people. They don't have the wherewithal to do it, even if they had the will. And I think it's a very people-intensive business model, in which every borrower is met week after week, because the repayments happen in very small amounts. To give an example, Rs. 5000 loan as a starting loan, and for 50 weeks you repay Rs. 100 every week. Now to be able to go to the doorstep of your borrower and be able to collect that Rs. 100 is a very massive exercise, it is entirely done with cash, I mean the amount of cash that goes in and out through the system, like I can talk about Spandana, that we have a presence in 12 states, our current portfolio would be over Rs. 4,000 crore and clients borrowers, close to 4.5 million, and a field staff of nearly 9,000 people work every day in terms of this kind of an outreach. So, 9,000 people are meeting for 4.5 million customers on a weekly basis, that's the kind of intensity that's required for this kind of business to be successful and viable, which somehow the formal banking sector never had the wherewithals to do it. So what banks in fact are required to support these sectors and it is part of Reserve Bank's requirement of priority sector lending, but since they cannot directly do it, they are lending to micro finance institutions, who in turn cater to these small borrowers, and these small borrowers, we must appreciate, are typically those who have been excluded from any financial services. In fact in such a large population of our country, only 40% or less have bank accounts.

It is all the more reason for the micro finance sector to reach out to that excluded sector. So, that, we are talking only about a bank account. Just because somebody has a bank account doesn't mean that he or she can get a loan. So if you look at the demand for finance, demand for loans and how many of them actually get it, the exclusion would be even higher as a percentage. So this is what I want you to appreciate as what the micro finance sector is doing and how it has evolved from a not-for-profit to very sustainable, extremely efficient, scalable business today. So these are the two basic broad understandings that we need to have and then let's come to the comparison, that why do we believe that micro finance would not have the kind of problems that subprime had. The only thing I see similar about the two is that they both cater to low income groups, that's why subprime is a word they use, that they are low income groups, they are not the prime borrowers of a bank. So low income is the only common thing everything else about the two lendings are completely different. First, is the way the credit decision is made. All the mortgage lending ultimately looks at the value of the collateral. So what is that property work and of course everyone thinks about the appreciation of that property. So against that, the lending takes place. Whereas in micro finance, all the lending is not — there is no collateral for a lending, it is only based on the cash flow. So, the approach to your credit decision is completely different.

And secondly, the capacity to repay, I think in a lot of US subprime mortgage, more and more loans were given to the same borrower, in other forms also, not just mortgage loans, but other loans, because as the value of that collateral kept moving up, in a consumerism-driven society, people reached out for more borrowings. It had more to do with the value of that house, value of the property, the collateral, and not so much to do with the cash flow. So, cash flow becomes the key determinant of how lending is done in micro finance. I have already mentioned that it is for a productive purpose, I mean home is very important to everyone, but at the end of the day, whatever money you put into it does not really generate any additional income, so that's the other difference that all micro finance lending eventually leads to additional income, additional cash flow for the borrower, and that is where the credit goes. The third is the customer contact. See whenever, like in the case of a subprime mortgage or any credit problem, a problem arises, usually a banker takes a long time before they find out about that problem, and this is not just when repayment starts, you know, getting into delinquency. The kind of customer contact that a credit officer in micro finance has on a week-to-week basis, even before there is likely to be any problem on repayments, he would know about it; because when you meet somebody on a weekly basis, interact in their own homes, you know exactly what the conditions are, what the problems are, so you get -- you are alerted of any likely problem very-very quickly, not after everything is over and now it's a problem. The other very unique feature that all micro finances generally, on the basis of a group and a joint liability to repay.

So whether it is an SHG or an MFI group, that group of 10 women or 5 women or whatever the model is, they take a joint responsibility to repay. So what happens is, today if I am one of the group members and I do not have my Rs. 100 to pay because my kid was sick or I had to pay the school fees or any reason, and I am short by Rs. 30, I had Rs. 70, but not Rs. 100, then maybe you who is also a group member, and who perhaps doesn't have similar needs in that week, will be able to help out. So this is the kind of concept where a whole group takes joint responsibility, though loans will be to individuals, so I may take Rs. 5,000, you may take Rs. 10,000, that may vary, but when it comes to repayment, we are all jointly responsible, and particularly in rural India, communities are very closely knit and they are very helpful to one another, and this kind of support within the group is always there, so there will be time when some member may not have adequate cash, but it never results in a default, because of this concept of group lending and group liability. So, that is other major difference. And another thing is also, as I mentioned earlier, this whole culture of saving, which is there in most developing countries and I can only talk of course about Indian experience. So even this problem about any difficulty, any additional cash flow requirement, not leading to repayment does not happen. People save and they are always generally able to repay. So these are some of the differences which are there and I think while some speakers may have talked about the high interest rates of the micro finance sector, it has to be looked at in the context of the weekly visit to every borrower, so the costs are incredibly high, but I am not saying that if it's possible to bring down the interest rate, it should be not passed on to borrowers, I am sure that can be done with greater efficiency and I don't know if there can be any technological intervention which is possible. But we must also appreciate, that one of the biggest reasons borrowers in US took huge housing loans beyond their needs, was because the interest rates were too low. And the second then, low interest rates is as much a problem.

And we must realize, this is something which when I interact with the domestic staff in our home, even though they may not be educated, they are quite savvy when it comes to the basic principles of money, which is very nice actually. So nobody will take a loan unless it is something which their cash flow is able to service, and there can be few people who may be tempted, I mean, unfortunately with this television culture and all that, I am sure the aspiration levels of even low income families, is moving up. But having said that, I think by and large the experience is that people don't borrow beyond what they need, and they don't borrow beyond what they are able to repay. So, perhaps a somewhat higher interest rate, becomes a deterrent to take unnecessary loan, which — just because it is so cheap, you take it, that kind of a mindset is not there. And people wonder that why is micro finance socially relevant, even though it has been commercialized? First of all, getting commercialized is not a bad thing, because for any activity to be viable, but for actual commercial capital coming into the sector, this kind of outreach that we are seeing today, could have never been achieved. People through NGOs would have still done very good work in small clusters and made an impact. Here, the impact is so much more.

Because micro finance is very efficient, because it has a fantastic track record of very low bad debts, and because there is a huge unmet demand for what they are offering, that is why the sector is in this huge growth phase currently, and whether there is commercial capital coming in or not, not relevant, because that capital is ultimately helping that same borrower, who needs that Rs. 5,000 to get her life started, to get that money and let me tell you, in so many interactions I have had, because I always make it like a annual pilgrimage to go to the villages where we work, to see how it really makes a difference. Savings in the hands of these women is invariably spent on education of children, health and hygiene, all these aspects, so it's not just money, it is complete transformation of the kind of life the family leads. And you should see some of these women, the kind of dignity that this work brings to them, they really can hold their heads high. So talking about woman empowerment and all, it's not as if, it doesn't happen, in fact, it is bound to happen. I mean it happens the same woman who may be not treated with respect, forget community, her own home, the way the family starts treating her because she contributes a significant amount of earnings, it just completely changes. So I mean, whatever maybe the source of capital, which fuels this growth, no one can take away the social impact that micro finance is creating.

Thank you,

■■■

6 Micro Finance: Maharashtra State Cooperative Bank Ltd., Experience

Mr. A.N. Wankhade,
Deputy Manager, Maharasthra
State Coop. Bank, Sector 17, Vashi.

Self-help Group: Way of Livelihood

Self-help Group (SHG) is the informal body of the people who come together to solve their common difficulties related to the financial needs. The concept of SHG popularized after the Introduction of Micro Credit through Gramin Bank in Bangladesh by Mohmod Yunus, an economist, around 1980s. In India, pilot project was launched by National Bank for Agriculture and Rural Development (NABARD) during 1992. In the State of Maharashtra, particularly in co-operative banks it took roots after inception of Maharashtra Rural Credit Project (MRCP) way back 1994. After its (MRCP) successful implementation and the lessons learnt, almost all banks and non-financing institutes have started looking towards SHG as a business proposal as it involves the minimal transaction cost, low cost deposit and large honest, creditworthy customer base. Some of the Non-government Organization (NGO) also joined their hand to NABARD as a partner of SHG-Bank Linkage Programme for effective implementation. The wholeheartily involvement and pioneering work done by them encourages the rural poor to enrich their life by way of poverty alleviation, bringing financial stability, creating awareness about their rights and developing leadership in them. NABARD provides financial assistance to its partners as a refinance against advances lent by them and also grants assistance on account of services they are providing to the SHGs. Government of Maharashtra (GoM) also took part in the process of poverty elevation through women's empowerment and providing interest subsidy to the Women's SHGs formed and nurtured under TEJSWINI programme. The interest subsidy is provided by the GoM through the Mahila Arthik Vikas Mahamandal (MAVIM, a GoM undertaking) @ 7% so as it reaches to SHGs up to 4% interest rate. The guiding principles for formation and linking of SHGs with banks, differ from banks to banks, but the normal features are as follows:

Formation of Group

The person who intends to form a group may call the people of similar socio-economic background in a small group and discuss with them about their common problems. Guide them how to overcome and also tell them about the importance of unity and saving. Also, make them aware of various schemes of government and the benefit that can be extracted. Meet them frequently till the group is formed, help them to be conversant with bank — to open the bank account. Now, most of people know the importance of SHG and hence, people, by themselves, form the group by adapting the other groups' experience. The task is easier for the entities who intend to form group.

Who Will be the Member of Group?

Only one member from the family can be the member of a group and cannot be member of two or more than two groups. This is required to avoid the dominance in the group. The groups are classified according to the member's characteristics, like gender based — male group, female group, mix group, based on income — below poverty line (BPL), above poverty line (APL) or based on the occupation, etc.

Bank Linkage

The group is saving linked as soon as it is formed. Saving Bank account is opened in the name of SHGs. The documents required includes resolution from the SHG signed by all members — deciding to open SB A/c with bank authorization from the SHG by the name of 2-3 members to operate the account jointly, Introduction, proof of residence, identity and photographs, copy of the rules and regulations.

The Characteristic of Ideal Group

The ideal group must possess following criteria:

1. Size of group: The size of group should be 10-20 members.
2. Meetings: Group should meet regularly. Ideally, meetings should be held weekly or fortnightly.
3. Compulsory attendance: Full attendance in all the group meetings helps SHG to stabilize.
4. Compulsory and regular savings/thrift.
5. Internal lending among members.
6. Maintenance of books of accounts.
7. Availing bank loan for onlending.
8. Discussing problems and finding solutions.
9. Group and social action.

Credit Linkage

Groups satisfying the above criteria and with an age of 6 months are eligible for credit linking. Banks have evolved their own criteria to ascertain the maturity and performing nature of groups. Based on the performance, weightage is given to each parameter and accordingly group is categorized. The parameter includes:

1. Age of the Group
2. Homogeneity of membership
3. Frequency and regularity of meeting
4. Attendance
5. Participation in meetings
6. Savings — frequency and regularity
7. Extent of utilization of savings
8. Loan repayment at SHG level

9. Books maintenance — accuracy and up-to-date
10. Knowledge of rules of the SHG
11. Decision-making and implementation thereof
12. Taking up Group and Social Action

Lending to SHG

Advances to SHGs are categorized as priority sector credit. Bank cannot insist for the security of consumption loan. Based on the performance of the group, loan is granted to the SHGs and not to individual members. Initially, loan is granted to meet the consumption needs of members. The quantum of loan is linked with the corpus (corpus includes gross saving, interest received, and other income including donations) of group in the ratio of 1:1 to 1:4. This quantum is indicative. Bank can extend higher loan, if the bank manager is satisfied with the need and also hopeful of recovery. After graduation and maturity of SHGs, subsequent loan doses are extended for the production purposes and the quantum is linked with financial viability of project.

Status

NABARD has launched SHGs-Bank Linkage Programme with 255 SHGs and now at national level, reaches to 9.7 crore household by way of saving linkage of 69.50 lakh SHGs and 48.5 lakh SHGs by way of credit linkage. The status during the year 2009-10 is as under:

Physical

Total number of SHGs savings linked with banks	:	69.53 lakh
Out of total [of which] exclusive Women SHGs	:	53.10 lakh
Out of total [of which] SGSY SHGs	:	16.94 lakh
Total number of SHGs credit linked during 2009-10	:	15.87 lakh
Out of total [of which] exclusive Women SHGs credit linked	:	12.94 lakh
Out of total [of which] SGSY SHGs credit linked	:	2.67 lakh
Total number of SHGs having loans outstanding as on 31st March, 2010	:	48.51 lakh
Of which exclusive Women SHGs	:	38.98 lakh
Of which-SGSY SHGs	:	12.45 lakh
Estimated number of families covered up to 31st March, 2010	:	9.7 core

Financial

Total savings amount of SHGs with banks as on 31st March, 2010	:	Rs. 6198.71 crore
Out of total savings of exclusive Women SHGs	:	Rs. 4498.66 crore
Out of total savings of SGSY SHGs	:	Rs. 1292.62 crore
Total amount of loans disbursed to SHGs during 2009-10	:	Rs. 14453.30 crore
Out of total loans disbursed to Women SHGs	:	Rs. 12429.37 crore
Out of total loans disbursed to SGSY SHGs	:	Rs. 2198.00 crore
Total amount of loans outstanding against SHGs on 31st March, 2010	:	Rs. 28038.28 crore
Out of total loans o/s against Women SHGs	:	Rs. 23030.36 crore
Out of total loans o/s against SGSY SHGs	:	Rs. 6251.08 crore
Average loan amount outstanding per SHG as on March 2010	:	Rs. 57795

State Level

In the state of Maharashtra, all banks together, were saving linked 770695 SHGs with gross saving of Rs. 56826.02 lakh and 110287 SHGs were credit linked amounting Rs.21284.24 lakh. The total outstanding against 384765 SHGs is Rs. 1203330.99 lakh. The share of Co-operative banks in linking of SHGs is higher than Commercial Banks and Regional Rural banks (RRBs) as can be seen from the following table:

Progress of SHG in the State of Maharashtra

(Amount in Rs. lakh)

Particulars	Saving		Credit Linkage		Outstanding	
	No. of Group	Amt	No. of Group	Amt	No. of Group	Amt
Commercial Banks	410864	29428.56	40742	30073.85	272010	92560.83
RRBs	91762	703.82	12768	2513.87	29482	11329.74
Co-operative Banks	268069	26695.64	56777	18696.52	83273	16440.42
Total	770695	56828.02	110287	51284.24	384765	120330.99

Source: NABARD Reports.

Role of Bank

Maharashtra State Co-operative Bank (MSCB) and District Central Co-operative Banks (DCCB) have recognized the involvement of women in shaping rural India and setting the pace of growth. This realization has lead to formation of Women Development Cell in MSCB as well as in DCCBs. Likewise, the concept and importance of SHG-Bank Linkage Programme which was launched by NABARD in 1992 was realized by the bank and implementing the same on massive scale through our constituents DCC Banks and Urban Banks in the state of Maharashtra. MSCB and DCC banks all together have formed around 2.42 lakh SHGs of which 2.40 lakh SHGs are saving linked.

Similarly, my bank has formulated a scheme for extending direct credit to SHGs in urban area through its branches. Bank has also formulated the refinance scheme exclusively for district level women co-operative societies of SHGs to enable them to extend finance to their women self-help groups; and another scheme for SHGs, their federations and societies to undertake the micro and small enterprises. In addition to this, bank has also taken initiative to provide marketing products of SHGs by way of organizing exhibitions. So far, the bank has organized three exhibition-cum-sale of SHGs products in its premises. The response from the participating SHGs and the visitors is encouraging.

Impact and Issues

SHG's Bank Linkage Programme launched by NABARD way back 1991-92 is regarded as an efficient tool for providing finance to the rural people and now acclaimed as a largest micro credit programme in the world. The impact of the programme and major issues are narrated below.

Impact:

1. SHG financing helps to provide credit accessibility to rural poor, who found that the formal credit delivery system is beyond their reach.
2. By virtue of being SHG members, the level of confidence, awareness and pride in them has increased among rural poor, especially women.
3. Banks benefit by the use of a cost-effective and efficient intermediary for raising deposits and advancing loans with a special advantage on the recovery front, which is above 90 per cent.

Major Issues:

1. Ensuring balanced growth in all the regions and intensifying efforts in the district where the progress is slow.
2. Intensifying efforts are to be taken by Co-operative banks for SHG credit linkage, as a large number of SHGs available with them.
3. Presently, interest subsidy scheme is applicable to the SHGs covered under Tejaswini programme. SHGs formed by various partners/agencies are to be covered under the scheme.
4. Strengthening of MIS.
5. The matured SHGs generally graduate from micro finance to micro enterprises.

■■■

7

Micro Finance: Myths and Realities

Mr. S. Chandrasekhar,
Senior Faculty, PNB Staff Training Collage

Micro Finance as a Step to Realize the Dream of a Healthy Nation*

Micro finance as we all understand is providing small quantum of amount as financial assistance to the poor. I do not understand the term VERY POOR as mentioned very often by many. POOR IS POOR and there is no need to further classify her/him as VERY POOR.

India has taken several measures to reach the poor with the sole purpose of uplifting the standard of living of the poor from BELOW THE POVERTY LINE TO ABOVE THE POVERTY LINE. The lines are crucial to classify them as POOR, VERY POOR, etc.

The Concept of Micro Finance is commendable and is highly acclaimed by world over which has been given a fillip by Bangladesh Noble Laureate Prof. Muhammad Yunus who started lending his own money to the poor villagers and succeeded in transforming them into successful entrepreneurs.

There are no reservations about uplifting the poor but in a country like ours where more than 60% population is Illiterate, the task is difficult though not impossible. With more than 60% of population not having a bank account and more than 75% not having access to Insurance our main endeavour should be to move

* S. Chandrashekhar, Sr. Faculty, PNB, RSC, Belapur, New Mumbai.

towards Financial Inclusion which needs to be done aggressively. Once they come into the banking fold, it is easy for us to educate them about small savings and micro finance. Even if we achieve the financial inclusion partially, we can take to Micro Financing and this project can be implemented by directly interacting with the needy poor with the help of Commercial Banks, Regional Rural Banks and Co-operative Banks. There are more than 5 crore families who have been financed through Micro financing.

Self-help Groups have played a major role in achieving the same, SHGs comprise 5 to 20 members in a group and they are educated and encouraged to save and contribute to a common fund meant for their own needy member. An individual is comfortable in a group (SHG) than be alone.

The Bankers need to have a Definite Policy of Micro Financing and should implement the same in true letter and spirit. The past experience of the bankers with SHGs is quite encouraging and the recovery percentage being quite high.

Though it is reported that Micro Financing Institutions are doing a commendable job in Micro Finance, our former RBI Governor Shri. Y.V. Reddy has been very critical about the MFIs, in fact, he opined "Micro Financing Institutions are worst than Moneylenders". Keeping the then RBI Governors remarks aside, it will be difficult for RRB's, Co-operative Banks and Commercial Banks alone to meet the requirements of the mass without the help of Micro Financing Institution.

I would like to conclude that Micro Finance to every poor person will be a reality in times to come and will have a long lasting effect on our economy culminating into a Healthy Nation which will be our DREAM.

■■■

Appendix

Andhra Pradesh Government's Ordinance on Micro Finance Institutions

Shri Hemanth Kumar,
Group Vice-President, Basix

An Ordinance to protect the women Self-help Groups from exploitation by the Micro Finance Institutions in the State of Andhra Pradesh and for the matters connected therewith or incidental thereto.

Whereas, Government of Andhra Pradesh has facilitated organization of the below poverty line households into self-help groups (SHGs) for the purpose of their economic advancement by achieving financial inclusion through linking with the banking network;

Whereas these SHGs are being exploited by private Micro Finance Institutions (MFIs) through usurious interest rates and coercive means of recovery resulting in their impoverishment and in some cases leading to suicides, it is expedient to make provisions for protecting the interests of the SHGs, by regulating the money lending transactions by the money lending MFIs and to achieve greater transparency in such transactions in the State of Andhra Pradesh;

And whereas, the Legislature of the State is not now in session and the Governor of Andhra Pradesh is satisfied that circumstances exists which render it necessary for him to take immediate action;

Now, therefore, in exercise of the powers conferred by clause (1) of Article 213 of the Constitution of India, the Governor hereby promulgates the following Ordinance:

Short title, extent and commencement	1. (1) This Ordinance may be called the Andhra Pradesh Micro Finance Institutions (Regulation of Money Lending) Ordinance, 2010. (2) It extends to the whole of the State of Andhra Pradesh. (3) It shall come into force at once. (4) It shall apply to Micro Finance Institutions whether they had come into existence before or after the commencement of this Ordinance.
Definitions	2. In this Ordinance, unless the context otherwise requires - (a) 'Self-help Group (SHG)' means a group of women formed on principles of self-help and registered as such with the Society for Elimination of Rural Poverty (SERP) in the rural areas or Mission for Elimination of Urban Poverty in Municipal Areas (MEPMA) in urban areas. (b) 'Society for Elimination of Rural Poverty (SERP)' is a Society formed by Government for the purpose of implementing pro-poor initiatives and thereby eliminating poverty in rural areas. (c) Society under 'Mission for Eliminating Poverty in Municipal Areas (MEPMA)' is a Society formed by Government for the purpose of implementing pro-poor initiatives and thereby eliminating poverty in urban areas. (d) 'Micro Finance Institution (MFI)' means any person, partnership Firm, group of persons, including a company registered under the provisions of the Companies Act 1956, a Non-banking Finance Company as defined under section 58-A of the Reserve Bank of India Act 1934, a Society registered under the A.P. Co-operative Societies Act 1964, or the A.P. Societies Registration Act 2001 and the like, in whichever manner formed and by whatever name called, whose principal or incidental activity is to lend money or offer financial support of whatsoever nature to the low income population. (e) 'Government' means the State Government of Andhra Pradesh. (f) 'SHG Bank Linkage' means provision of credit for the SHGs by the commercial banks based on a micro credit plan prepared by the SHGs for carrying out economic activities. (g) 'Interest' for the purposes of the terms defined under the provisions of this Ordinance would mean a return on the amount lent by the MFI to a SHG.

	(h) 'Loan' means an advance whether of money or in kind given to the borrowing SHG at interest, whether given before the commencement of this Act or after such commencement and includes advance, discount, money paid for or on account of or paid on behalf of or at the request of any person, or any account whatsoever, and every agreement (whatever its terms or form may be) which is in substance or effect a loan of money or in kind given to an SHG and further includes, an agreement relating to the repayment of any such loan. (i) 'Notification' means a notification published in the Andhra Pradesh Gazette and the word 'notified' shall be construed accordingly. (j) 'Prescribed' means prescribed by Rules made under this Ordinance. (k) 'Registering Authority' means the Project Director District Rural Development Agency for the rural areas and Project Director MEPMA for urban areas; or any other person appointed by the District Collector to perform the functions of a registering authority under this Ordinance for such District. (l) 'Registration' means registration granted to a MFI under this Ordinance. (m) "SHG Member" means a registered member of a SHG who intends to avail a loan through such SHG. (n) Words used but not defined in this Ordinance, shall have the same meaning assigned under the relevant Acts.
Registration of MFIs	3. (i) All MFIs operating in the State of Andhra Pradesh as on the date of the commencement of this Ordinance, shall within thirty days from the date of commencement of this Ordinance, apply for Registration before the Registering Authority of the district specifying therein the villages or towns in which they have been operating or propose to operate, the rate of interest being charged or proposed to be charged, system of conducting due diligence and system of effecting recovery and list of persons authorized for conducting the activity of lending or recovery of money which has been lent. (ii) No MFIs, operating at the commencement of this Ordinance or intending to start the business of lending money to SHGs, after the commencement of this Ordinance, shall grant any loans or recover any loans without obtaining registration under this Ordinance from the Registering Authority.

	(iii) The Registering Authority shall conduct verification of the details furnished by the MFI and accord registration in such manner as may be prescribed for operation of MFIs for a period of one year, after obtaining a written undertaking from the MFI that it shall always act in conformity with the provisions of this Ordinance. (iv) Where the MFI applies for renewal of registration, an application for that purpose shall be filed by the MFI 60 days before the expiry of the period of one year referred to in sub-section (3) and the Registering Authority shall decide either to grant renewal or refuse renewal of registration within 15 days before the date of expiry of registration, after due verification of the performance of the MFIs in the field level and after hearing objections, if any, from the general public regarding extension of Registration.
Register of MFIs	4. (i) Every registering authority shall maintain for the area under its jurisdiction registers of all MFIs having valid registration in such form as may be prescribed. (ii) The registers maintained under sub-section (1) shall be published in such manner and at such intervals as may be prescribed.
MFIs to obtain registration	5. (i) The Registering Authority may, at any time, either *suo moto* or upon receipt of complaints by SHGs or its members or by members of the public cancel the registration of an MFI after assigning sufficient reasons for such cancellation. Provided that no order of cancellation of the Registration shall be passed without issuing notice to the MFI intimating the facts upon which the *prima facie* decision to cancel the registration has been taken and the MFI shall be afforded a reasonable opportunity to show cause against such notice. **Explanation:** For the purposes of sub-section (1), conviction of a MFI for an offence of violation of any of the provisions of this Ordinance shall be sufficient cause for suspension or cancellation of its registration. (ii) Pending enquiry under sub-section (1), the Registering Authority may, for sufficient reasons to be recorded, suspend the Registration of an MFI.
Member of SHG not to be member of more than one SHG	6. No member of an SHG shall be a member of more than one SHG, provided that where a member has, at the commencement of this Ordinance, become a member of more than one SHG, she shall have the option to retain the membership of one SHG and to terminate her membership in other SHGs and for that purpose, she shall issue a notice to such SHGs about her option to terminate her membership, settle and pay the amount payable to the

		MFIs which had lent monies to such SHGs, within a period of 3 months from the date of commencement of this Ordinance.
MFIs not to seek security	7.	No MFI shall seek any security from a borrower by way of pawn, pledge or other security for the loan. Provided that any such security obtained from a borrower before the commencement of this Ordinance shall forthwith stand released in favour of the borrower.
Display of rates of interest charged by MFIs	8. (i)	All MFIs shall display the rates of interest charged by them in a conspicuous place in their premises in bold letters visible to the members of the public.
	(ii)	No MFI shall charge any other amount from the borrower except any charge prescribed in the Rules for submission of an application for grant of a loan.
Maximum amount of interest recoverable on loans and discharge of loans in certain cases	9. (i)	No MFI shall recover from the borrower towards interest in respect of any loans advanced by it, whether before or after commencement of this Ordinance, an amount in excess of the principal amount.
	(ii)	All loans in respect of which an MFI has realized from the borrower, whether before or after commencement of this Ordinance, an amount equal to twice the amount of the principal, shall stand discharged and the borrower shall be entitled to obtain refund and the MFI shall be bound to refund the excess amount paid by the borrower.
Prior approval for grant of further loans to SHGs or their members	10. (1)	No MFI shall extend a further loan to a SHG or its members, where the SHG has an outstanding loan from a Bank unless the MFI obtains the prior approval in writing in such manner as may be prescribed from the Registering Authority after making an application seeking such approval.
	(2)	The Registering Authority while considering such application from an MFI seeking approval as aforesaid, shall secure the following information in writing from the MFI in regard to every member of SHG namely, (i) Name of the Borrower (ii) Name of the SHG (iii) bank from which loan has been obtained by the SHG (iv) date of the loan granted by the bank (v) amount paid to the SHG by the bank (vi) amount due from the SHG

	(vii) fresh amount of loan sought by the SHG from the MFI (viii) terms of repayment proposed by the MFI (ix) details of due diligence including the capacity of the SHG for repayment and (x) such other details as may be prescribed by Rules made under this Ordinance. (3) The Registering Authority shall, not later than fifteen days from the date of filing of such application for approval under subsection (2), cause an enquiry into the contents of the application and shall grant approval for further loan unless the Registering Authority is satisfied that the SHG and its members have passed a resolution that they have understood the conditions of the loan and terms of repayment and unless the Registering Authority is also satisfied that such further loan would generate additional income to the SHG and its members, needed for servicing the debt. (4) No MFI shall grant loan to a member of SHG during the subsistence of two previous loans irrespective of the source of the previous two loans.
Duty of MFIs to maintain accounts and furnish copies	11. (1) All borrowings by a member of an SHG from an MFI shall be contracted in the manner, form and format prescribed under the Ordinance. (2) Every MFI shall keep and maintain a cash book, a ledger and such other books of account in such form and in such manner as may be prescribed. (3) Every MFI shall- (a) Deliver or cause to be delivered, to the borrower within seven days from the date on which a loan is made, a statement in the prescribed form showing in clear and distinct terms the amount and date of the loan and of its maturity, the name and address of the functionary of the MFI and the effective rate of interest charged. (b) Upon repayment of a loan in full, the MFI shall obtain an indelible mark on every paper signed by the borrower with words indicating such repayment and provide copies thereof to the borrower. (4) No MFI shall receive any payment from a borrower on account of any loan without giving him a duly signed receipt for the payment. (5) An MFI shall, on a demand in writing by the borrower, supply a copy of any document relating to a loan obtained

		by him, or if the borrower so requires, to any person specified in that behalf in the demand. Provided that in respect of loans given prior to the commencement of this Ordinance, it shall be obligatory for the lender to specify if any security was accepted from the borrower.
	(6)	All tranches of repayment shall be made by the group at the office of the Gram Panchayat only.
	(7)	MFI shall not deploy any agents for recovery nor shall use any other coercive action either by itself or by its agents for recovery of money from the borrower; and any form of coercive recovery including but not limited to visiting the house of the borrower shall, apart being punishable under the provisions of the Ordinance, empower the Registering Authority to suspend or cancel the license of such an MFI as provided in Section 5.
Submissions of monthly statement by MFIs	12.	Every MFI shall submit a Monthly Statement to the Registering Authority before 10th day of every month giving therein the list of borrowers, the loan given to each and the interest rate charged on the repayment made.
Power to require production of records or documents and power of entry, inspection and seizure	13. (1)	The Registering Authority or any officer authorised by him in this behalf may, to verify whether the business of the MFI is being carried on in accordance with the provisions of this Ordinance, enter the premises of the MFI office or of any person who in his opinion is carrying on the business of lending and call upon him to produce any record or document relating to such business and every such MFI shall allow such inspection and produce such record or document.
	(2)	The Registering Authority may, for the purposes of sub-section (1), search the premises and seize any record and document as may be necessary and the record or document seized shall be retained only for such period as may be necessary for the purposes of examination, prosecution or other legal action. Provided that the provisions of Sections 100 and 102 of the Code of Criminal Procedure, 1973 shall, so far as may be, apply to such search and seizure.
	(3)	The registering authority or the other officer referred to in sub-section (1) shall also have power to summon and examine the MFI or any person who in his opinion is in a position to furnish relevant information.
Complaints	14.	Any SHG or its members or any member of the public can file a complaint regarding violation of the provision of this

	Ordinance by a MFI before the Registering Authority and the said Authority shall enquire into the same after giving a reasonable opportunity to the MFI to show cause and pass such orders as it may deem fit including an order under section 5 of the Ordinance.
Settlement of Disputes	15. (1) For the protection of debtors and for the settlement of disputes of civil nature between the SHG or its members on the one hand and the MFI on the other hand or between the members of the SHG and the SHG, in relation to the loans granted under this Ordinance to the SHG or its members, the State Government after consultation with the High Court, and by notification,- (a) Shall, as soon as may be after the commencement of this Ordinance, establish for every district in the State a Fast-Track Court; (b) May establish Fast-Track Court for such other areas in the State, as it may deem necessary. (2) The Government shall, after consultation with the High Court of Andhra Pradesh specify, by notification, the local limits of the area to which the jurisdiction of a Fast-Track Court shall extend and may, at any time, increase, reduce or alter such limits. (3) The cases that may be filed before the Fast-Track Court shall be disposed of within a period of three months. (4) The decree of the Fast-Track Courts shall be liable to be executed in accordance with the procedure under the Code of the Civil Procedure 1908.
Penalty for coercive actions by MFIs	16. (1) All persons who are connected with and responsible for the day-to-day control, business and management of a MFI including the Partners, Directors and the employees who resort to any type of coercive measures against the SHGs or its members of their family members shall be liable for punishment of imprisonment which may extend up to a period of three years or with fine which may extend to one lakh rupees or with both. **Explanation:** For the purposes of this section, "coercive action" by an MFI against the SHGs or its members of their family members include the following- (a) obstructing or using violence to, insulting or intimidating the borrower or his family members, or (b) persistently following the borrower or his family member from place to place or interfering with any property owned or used by him or depriving him of, or hindering him in, the use of any such property

		(c) frequenting the house or other place where such other person resides or works, or carries on business, or happens to be, or (d) doing any act calculated to annoy or intimidate such person or the members of his family, or (e) moving or acting in a manner which causes or is calculated to cause alarm or danger to the person or property of such other person, or (f) seeking to remove forcibly any document from the borrower which entitles the borrower to a benefit under any Government programme. Provided that a person who frequents the house or place referred to in clause (c) in order merely to obtain or communicate information shall not be deemed to be using coercive action.
	(2)	The MFI or the persons who use coercive actions as stated in sub-section (1) shall be prosecuted in accordance with the provisions of this Ordinance.
	(3)	The provisions of the Code of Criminal Procedure, 1973, shall, so far as may be, apply to the proceedings before a Fast Track Court, and for the purpose of the said provisions, a Fast Track Court shall be deemed to be a Magistrate.
Penalty for carrying on business without registration	17.	All persons who are connected with and responsible for the day-to-day control, business and management of a MFI including the Partners and Directors of such MFI which carries on the business of providing loans either without obtaining registration of the MFI from the Registering Authority under Section 3 of the Ordinance, shall be liable for punishment with imprisonment for a term which may extend to three years and with fine which may extend to rupees one lakh.
Penalty for contravention of the provisions of the Ordinance	18.	If any person contravenes any provision other than Section 3 of this Ordinance, he shall be punishable with imprisonment for a period of six months or with fine which may extend to ten thousand rupees or with both.
Every officer to be public servant	19.	Every officer of the Government and every person acting under the provisions of this Ordinance shall be deemed to be a public servant within the meaning of Section 21 of the Indian Penal Code.
Bar of certain proceedings	20. (1)	No suit, prosecution or other proceedings shall lie against any officer or employee of the Government for any act done or purporting to be done under this Ordinance, without the previous sanction of the Government.

		(2) No suit, prosecution or other legal proceedings shall be instituted against any person for anything which is, in good faith, done or intended to be done under this Ordinance or the rules made thereunder.
Power to remove difficulties	21.	If any difficulty arises in giving effect to the provisions of this Ordinance, the Government may, by notification, remove difficulties by orders not inconsistent with the provisions of this Ordinance, but which appear to them to be necessary or expedient to remove such difficulty.
Power to give directions	22.	The Government may, from time to time, issue such orders, instructions and directions not inconsistent with the provisions of this Ordinance and the rules made thereunder to the officers for the proper administration of the Ordinance, and such officers and all other persons employed in the enforcement of the Ordinance, shall comply with such orders, instructions and directions.
Power to make rules	23.	(1) The State Government may, by notification, make rules for carrying out the purposes of this Ordinance. (2) Every rule made under this Ordinance shall, immediately after it is made, be laid before the Legislature of the State, if it is in session and if it is not in session, in the session immediately following for a total period of fourteen days which may be comprised in one session or in two successive sessions and if, before the expiration of the session in which it is so laid or the session immediately following the Legislature agrees in making any modification in the rule or in the annulment of the rule, the rule shall, from the date on which the modification or annulment is notified, have effect only in such modified form or shall stand annulled as the case may be so, however, that any such modification or annulment shall be without prejudice to the validity of anything previously done under that rule.
Annual Report on the administration of the Ordinance	24.	The Government shall prepare an annual report on the administration of this Ordinance and the same shall be placed before the State Legislature.

Statement of Objects and Reasons

The Government of Andhra Pradesh has made rapid strides in the field of financial inclusion of the rural and urban poor by organizing women self-help groups (SHGs); and linking them with the banks for meeting their credit needs.

Of late, many individuals and entities have come up styling themselves as Micro Finance Institutions and are giving loans to SHGs at very high or usurious rates of interest and are using inhuman coercive methods for recovery of the loans.

This has even resulted in suicides by many rural poor who have obtained loans from such individuals or entities. In the larger public interest and to protect the poor from exploitation, and to regulate the lending of monies to the SHGs by the MFIs, the Government intends to bring into force a law containing the various provisions stated in this Bill in order to check the illegal acts of these MFIs.

This Bill seeks to give effect to the above decision.

■■■